"Henry Hutcheson has truly captured the essence of the pros and cons, ups and downs, and good and bad of running a family business."

—*Mercer F. Stanfield*, president and COO, Brame Specialty Company, fourth-generation family business

"A wake-up call for family business leaders, family members in the business, and the trusted advisors of the family business. Henry Hutcheson brings up difficult situations, but always with a light touch, that are worthy of examination."

—*Rhonda Stokes*, interim director, Wake Forest University Family Business Center, Triad, and Charlotte Centers

"Henry Hutcheson has captured not only the complex issues between the family and their family-owned business, but has also identified the critical steps needed to succeed beyond the first generation."

—*Chris Cecil*, president, Biltmore Family Office, LLC

"Henry simplifies complex family business matters, focuses on what is most important to family members, and provides answers that people can take home and use right now."

—*Cindy Clarke*, executive director, UNC, Asheville Family Business Forum

"Henry Hutcheson has a deep understanding of how small businesses survive generational transfers and how they don't. Moreover, he has a rare ability to explain the complexities of those transfers in clear and understandable language. This book is a must-read for anyone who hopes their business will not only survive but also thrive long after they are gone."

—*Whit Ayres*, president and owner,
North Star Opinion Research

"This book captures the critical issues and the steps that family businesses need to follow to maintain profitability and sanity."

—*Lisa Oswald*, CEO, Sorrelli

Dirty Little Secrets of
Family
Business

ENSURING SUCCESS FROM
ONE GENERATION TO THE NEXT

Henry Hutcheson, CMC, CFBA

RIVER GROVE
BOOKS

Published by River Grove Books
Austin, TX
www.rivergrovebooks.com

Distributed by River Grove Books

Design and composition by Greenleaf Book Group and Sheila Parr
Cover design by Greenleaf Book Group and Sheila Parr
Cover image: ©Shutterstock.com/Murvin, ©iStockphoto.com/artsstock

Publisher's Cataloging-in-Publication data is available.

Paperback ISBN: 978-1-63299-590-2

eBook ISBN: 978-1-62634-261-3

Third Edition, Trade Paperback

Originally published as 978-1941870006,
Indie Books International, LLC, Oceanside, CA
978-1-62634-260-6, Greenleaf Book Group Press

This book is dedicated to three people: Warren Hutcheson, Dennis Gile, and Giovanni Agnelli—great friends of mine who were each on a path to change the world, but whose lives were unfortunately cut short. They left a hole in the families and communities they came from and will always be missed.

Contents

Acknowledgments

This book is a compilation of many years of work, tremendous research, and extensive engagements helping family businesses find the answers that are best for them. While academicians, business leaders, and professionals can all gain insights from *Dirty Little Secrets of Family Business*, its true audience is anyone currently running a family business and anyone in the next generation who may one day be running the family business. Thus, while each chapter attempts to address the various broad questions facing all family businesses, the perspective does shift back and forth between these two viewpoints.

Clearly none of this would have been possible without a lot of help. I would like to thank the Family Firm Institute (FFI) and members, my Institute of Management Consultants (IMC), the Society of Financial Services Professionals, the Wake Forest family business program, the editors of all the McClatchy papers, IGC and its members, the Psychodynamics of Family Business group, and the Kure Beach Professional Society.

On a personal level, let me thank my brother Jim, who brought me into the family business profession and showed me the ropes; Jane Hilburt-Davis, my FFI mentor; and Dane Huffman, who helped me break into the professional writing field. Let me, of course, thank my family: Oskar, Avery, and Kirsten, for their patience with my travel schedule, and Kirsten in particular for her many hours of editing. Finally, this book truly would not have been possible without those family business owners and members with whom I have spent so much time; I offer a special thanks to Eddie, Mark, Kevin, Kayle, Mercer, Lisa, Kermit, and Lily.

Introduction

"Happy families are all alike; every unhappy family is unhappy in its own way." So begins Leo Tolstoy's classic novel, *Anna Karenina*. The same is true for the unhappy family business; every unhappy family business is unhappy in its own way. The root causes of the unhappiness, and the solutions, are the dirty little secrets of family business.

Family businesses form the backbone of the economy in the United States and virtually every country of the world. The Family Firm Institute (FFI) estimates that more than 70 percent of all businesses are family businesses. At the same time, family businesses historically have accounted for the largest portion of new jobs created, a significant percentage of the gross domestic product (GDP), and a good chunk of Fortune 500 companies.

"Happy families are all alike; every unhappy family is unhappy in its own way."

What is a family business exactly? Some people define it as simply two or more relatives working in the same company. Another school of thought attributes family business status when there is significant family influence. Many think that "family business" simply means *small business.* But billion-dollar companies such as Ford, Walmart, and Cargill would disagree. The best definition I have encountered comes from Carmen Bianchi, the director of the Family Business Center at San Diego State University, who defines a family business as "any business that considers itself to be a family business."

There are also definitions of the generations of a family business. The first generation is referred to as the "founding generation," the second as a "sibling partnership," and the third as a "cousins' consortium." I usually refer to the fourth generation as "Wow, isn't that amazing," because only a small percentage of diligent and forward-thinking family businesses ever make it that far.

Family businesses, like relatives, come in many shapes and sizes. Most family businesses begin with a single founder, who either saw an opportunity or simply took action to make ends meet. Maybe it was both. However, this situation can quickly turn into a husband and wife team, or two siblings. Many family businesses are owned and run by women, who have the additional burden and conflict of being mom and the chief emotional support for the family.

Then the next generation comes along, grows up among the hustle and bustle of their parents trying to build a business, helps out where possible, and one day finds that they are working in their parents' business. Then the kids get married and bring in-laws into the business. Trusted and capable nonfamily employees are picked up along the way.

Regardless of the definition or form, there can be no greater joy than working with the people you love the most. But family businesses can also be challenging. Family is about unconditional love, and business is about profit.

These two goals do not always align. You may love your child, but maybe he is not cut out to run the business. You may love your father, but maybe he is getting ready to make a bad investment. Your child may not be qualified for a position, but because you love him and don't want to hurt his feelings or self-esteem, you give him the position.

According to FFI research, two out of three family businesses do not survive into the next generation. And not just from the first generation to the second, but from any generation to the next.

A lot of information is available on what the central causes are for family business failures—and thus, some guidelines on how to avoid them. In this book we address the top success strategies for family businesses to survive and even thrive. Briefly, here are the key rules:

- **Keep the lines of communication open.** Communication is critical; otherwise minor issues can fester and become much more challenging problems.
- **Assign clear roles and responsibilities.** There is a natural tendency for family members involved with their family's business to think everything is their business. However, not everything is every family member's responsibility. Without job definitions, family members will be on top of each other trying to solve the same problem.
- **Keep good financial data.** The downfall of many small businesses and family businesses is not having solid data. Good financial data is like a clean windshield: It lets you know exactly where you are.
- **Avoid overpaying family members.** Market-based compensation is fundamental and essential. Parents

in family businesses tend to overpay the next generation, or pay all family members the same. Both
are bad practices. The longer unfair compensation
practices continue, the messier it is to clean up when
it blows up.

- **Don't hire relatives if they are unqualified.** Family
  businesses are a conundrum: The family aspect generates unqualified love, while the business side cares
  about profits. Thus family members may be given a
  job even when they are not qualified. The remedy
  is to get them trained and move them to a role that
  matches their skills, or have them leave.

High-functioning family businesses can outperform
nonfamily businesses on a number of metrics. Trust is the
driver. But when trust breaks down, the business suffers,
placing a significant strain on family harmony. Adhering to
the five key rules, while uncomfortable, can keep a family
and business on the track to success and help it avoid being
one of those that does not survive.

This book is intended to fill an unmet need: convey
actions and ways of thinking to all family business members on how to have a well-run, harmonious family business. *Dirty Little Secrets of Family Business* is written in
a style and manner that is purposely readable and understandable to family business members. Moreover, it uses
multiple examples of successful and unsuccessful family
businesses to demonstrate the application and effectiveness
of the information.

By reading this book, you can build an implementable
plan to address any family business situation you may

encounter, which enables you to come through tough times with a better-functioning business and family members who happily spend holidays and vacations together.

CHAPTER 1

How Are Family Businesses Different?

Having a family business is a wonderful advantage. You control your destiny, you can invest for the long term, and it can be a tremendous resource for the next generation, whether it provides work experience for them to get jobs elsewhere, work within the family business, or is simply a financial resource to care for the well-being of your family. If you have a family business, it is important to work hard—and smart—to ensure its success from one generation to the next.

You would think family businesses matter because there are a lot of them, and you would be correct. As I mentioned in the introduction, more than 70 percent of all businesses are family businesses, and they account for a significant number of new jobs and a large portion of GDP. However, what is perhaps more important is that so many are being created every day. With more than 500,000 new businesses starting each month in the United States,[1] the genesis of thousands of family businesses occurs every day.

Warren Buffett, arguably the world's greatest investor,

---

1 Jason Nazar, "16 Surprising Statistics About Small Businesses," *Forbes*, Sept. 9, 2013, http://www.forbes.com/sites/jasonnazar/2013/09/09/16-surprising-statistics-about-small-businesses.

touched on his passion for family businesses in his February 27, 2009, letter to shareholders: "Our long-avowed goal is to be the 'buyer of choice' for businesses—particularly those built and owned by families . . . We have a decided advantage, therefore, when we encounter sellers who truly care about their businesses."[2] If Warren Buffett thinks family businesses matter, who are we to argue?

[M]ore than 70 percent of all businesses are family businesses, and they account for a significant number of new jobs and a large portion of GDP.

What Makes Family Businesses Special?

We must also understand that family businesses are different and unique from nonfamily businesses. In a family business there is a permanent emotional relationship with your work colleagues. Families are lifelong social structures, characterized by unqualified love and support among their members. You can quit your job, but you can't quit your family.

This brings us to another great statistic of family businesses: Many studies have shown that family businesses outperform nonfamily businesses. The reasons for this phenomenon are plentiful. Yes, people try harder when the

2 http://www.berkshirehathaway.com/letters/2008ltr.pdf.

family name is on the sign. Yes, family businesses have a longer-term perspective than the quarterly driven, publicly held nonfamily businesses. And yes, you can use your kids as slave labor and get away with it!

But the number-one factor that enables family businesses to rise to the top is the level of trust. Each family member involved in a successful family business knows that every other member is doing their best to move the company forward. Professor John Whitney of Columbia Business School stated in his book, *The Trust Factor* (New York: McGraw-Hill, 1994), "Imagine the performance of your company if everyone knew what, when, and how to do everything, did it correctly and on time, all in alignment with the company mission." Family businesses, because of the inherent closeness of the family members, can have such a high trust level that everyone can be perfectly synchronized in their work efforts, bringing about a highly successful business.

Dirty Little Secret: The number-one factor that enables family businesses to rise to the top is the level of trust.

But what happens when trust breaks down? Or when one family member is not willing or able to perform at the requisite level? Perhaps it is because of a sense of entitlement, drug abuse, or simple laziness. Any of these could force the other family members to pretend to ignore the problem or ask the profoundly awkward question, "How do I fire my son/daughter/brother/sister?" The former is bad for business, and the latter is bad for the family.

This is the reason professionalizing the family business early is so important. (See page 87 near the end of chapter 4.) It helps move the business in the right direction while removing the inherent personal nature of a family business. However, it can be difficult. To survive and grow, decisions must be made quickly and chances must be taken. Making mistakes is unavoidable. Once a level of success and stability is achieved, there usually is no manual on how to run the business because it is all in the founder's head.

Nonetheless, for a family business to be successful long term, it must put forth the effort in some key areas: communication, governance, management succession, and planning.

Fortunately there is help, such as publications like *Family Business Magazine* and *Family Business Journal*. Family businesses can join university-based family business centers around the country that put useful programming together for their members by bringing in outside expert speakers, facilitating sessions on meaningful topics, and bringing family business research results to the group. There is also the Family Firm Institute, the leading association worldwide for family enterprise professionals. The institute is dedicated to being a resource for family businesses and providing education and certification to those who serve family businesses.

And then there are, of course, family business consultants who assist these businesses with their issues, like our firm, Family Business USA. Our firm was founded on the idea that family businesses can benefit from getting professional help. How did I first learn of the dirty little secrets of family business? I grew up working for my family's business, Olan Mills Portrait Studios, the predominant provider of family photography throughout the United States.

My grandfather, Olan Mills, founded the company. My two uncles took it over for the next generation. While my brother seemed happy working in our family business, I decided to make my own path by pursuing a global management career with IBM.

Where Will Our Children Work?

I recently attended my twentieth reunion at Columbia Business School. For two days we listened to lectures delivered by prominent professors and distinguished alumni. While the sessions covered a variety of topics, one theme dominated the weekend: Where will the jobs come from in the future? Professor Bruce Greenwald, touted as one of the top finance professors in the country, began his lecture by saying, "You all had better get used to your kids living at home with you for a long time to come." He then went on to describe the enormous imbalance in savings rates between those with the top 20 percent of income versus the bottom 80 percent. That bottom 80 percent is actually at a negative savings rate.

Diving even deeper, Andrew L. Stern, senior fellow at the Columbia Richard Paul Richman Center and presidential appointee to the Simpson-Bowles commission, stated it more bluntly: "If anyone has an idea where our kids and grandkids are going to work in the future, please let me know." Through the course of his lecture he displayed a terrifying graph. Essentially, it showed that since 1940, GDP, productivity, and wages have increased every year until 2004, when they started diverging. Employment also remained steady through these years but began diverging in 2008. We believe the cause for this divide is the subprime mortgage debacle. While it compounded the problem, the real cause is technology. We are replacing jobs with technology at such a rate that there simply will not be enough jobs to go around in the future on a global basis. That's right—*global* basis. In Europe there are fast-food restaurants where an ATM takes your order. How long will it take before they are in Bangladesh? Beijing? Dubai? Boston? Three-D printers can make automotive parts, camera lenses, coffee cups, prosthetics, and even human tissue. How long will it take until everything is simply printed?

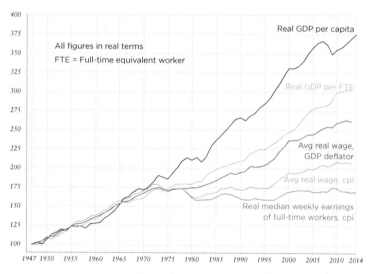

Figure 1.1 From GDP per Capita to Median Wage
1947 to 2013/14, 1947 = 100

Sources: BEA and BLS, 2015

In the 2015 July/August edition of *The Atlantic* magazine, Derek Thompson took the issue further in the article
"A World Without Work," stating that machines might be
able to take half of all US jobs in two decades. Case in
point, in 1964 AT&T was worth $267 billion in today's
dollars and employed 758,611 people, but Google is now
worth $370 billion and employs a mere 55,000 workers.[3]

Year	Company	Worth	Employees
1964	AT&T	$267 billion	758,611
2015	Google	$370 billion	55,000

Advantages of Owning a Family Business

Owning your own business is a big advantage in a world
where technology is eliminating jobs at an unprecedented
rate. Yes, you can sell your business, and sometimes that is
the best or only alternative. But selling your business simply
changes the business you are in: Whereas once you were a
business operator, after the sale you become a money manager. The differences between the two are stark: As a business operator you have great experience that can be passed
on, and your efforts can be directly tied to the performance
of the business, but as a money manager you are not an
expert by definition and, regardless of your efforts, are held
captive to unknown global market forces. Unless you are

---

3 Derek Thompson, "A World Without Work," *The Atlantic*, July/August
  2015.

in a dying industry, are being offered well above what your business is worth, or simply have no heirs, owning a business is a wonderful advantage.

As a family business owner, you can control your destiny because your income is derived specifically from your own personal effort, intelligence, creativity, and management skills. Granted, some people are better at running certain businesses than others, and some people simply are not cut out to run a business. Nonetheless, perhaps you would make a good owner and could learn to effectively manage the person who does run the business. Maybe you could be an effective chairman of the board, but not the CEO.

The flip side to this is selling the business. Once it is sold, you essentially become an investor. Better said, you become someone who manages investors. This can certainly be done. However, you have much less control over your destiny. The people managing your money can turn over, their performance can fluctuate, and of course, the market itself can fluctuate—many times—for unexpected reasons. So while we may all get excited about converting the family business into cash, you really are just moving into another business called investing, where you may have little experience and will definitely have less control.

Owning a family business is also a great resource for giving the next generation a leg up. When you own a family business, you can plug your kids straight into some fairly meaningful work experience at a young age—in sales, administration, production, or even general office work. This work experience helps develop a good work ethic and the ability to work with others further down the road. Additionally, the work experience can be listed on a resume and be used to leverage into other better jobs with other companies. When I graduated from college, I had a fairly impressive resume with jobs that all extended from my time at Olan Mills. I have seen the children of multiple family businesses parlay their family business work experience into good starter jobs in other companies. And many times this work experience at a young age simply turns into making your child a great candidate to work at the family business long term.

> **Dirty Little Secret:** Having a family business is a wonderful advantage.

Finally, while there are myriad financial instruments out there to assist in the transition of wealth down through the generations, having ownership in a company enables the family to plan long term for investments and development of personnel. A well-run company can serve as a financial resource for the benefit of future generations.

Case Study: Apex Family

Have you ever seen people hanging from the sides of buildings, cleaning windows fifty floors up? Did you think: Those people are crazy? If you got to know Scotties Building Services, the tenth-largest window-cleaning company in the country, and a family business, you would quickly realize they know exactly what they are doing.

Scotties is truly a rags-to-riches story. Back in 1986, John McGrath, who grew up working in the window-cleaning business with his dad in Syracuse, New York, decided to get out of the snow and moved south to North Carolina. Once he was settled, he sent for his dad. Soon after, his brother Tom left the military and joined them in forming a new window-cleaning business.

The window-cleaning business was different back then. "It was like the Wild West," John McGrath said. "Some crazy guys with a bucket of soap and a wiper could get jobs hanging off buildings, cleaning. It's not like that anymore." Today, the business has professionalized. The time when someone with a bucket of soap could get a job is gone. Scotties saw this change and professionalized themselves and their business.

John and Tom McGrath were founding members of the International Window Cleaning Association, whose charter is to promote safety and education and enhance professionalism throughout the industry. Scotties went about cleaning up the cleaning industry. And the family led by example by professionalizing themselves. A lot of this came about by reading a book, *The E-Myth* (New York: HarperBusiness, 1990), by Michael Gerber.

"The point of *The E-Myth* is to spend time working *on* your business, not just *in* your business," Tom McGrath said. "It teaches you how to put systems and controls in place, and that's what we did at Scotties."

The cleaning industry has low barriers to entry, and there are no legal certifications required to operate. The key to success is to be safe, efficient, economical, and consistent. In fact, this is the company's motto. Developing a reputation is the key to success. With a 96 percent retention rate, it looks like it is paying off.

The McGraths' dedication to safety extended so far

that they formed another company focusing exclusively on designing and manufacturing safety harnesses for high-rise building cleaners.

The key to success is to be safe, efficient, economical, and consistent.

The McGrath family also has spent time working on being a high-performing family business. They have divided the functional areas among the three of them with John in charge of sales and marketing, Tom focusing on management and operations, and Dad providing the initial expertise required to safely and thoroughly clean the windows of tall buildings. It is a known family business management tenet that the clearer the definition of roles and responsibilities, the better.

But what happens when disagreements occur? "We talk it out," Tom said, "but ultimately the decision falls to the one who has responsibility for that particular area, and we just trust each other." What also helps is a strong staff. Scotties has four geographic divisions with a general manager running each who has a great deal of autonomy. "Having a strong management team provides another good source of input for decision making," Tom said.

Another trick they learned to help them work well together as a family business is that they try to keep business talk to business hours. And they consciously avoid taking on issues toward the end of the workday. "Any issues that come up late in the day, we just save them for tomorrow," John said.

Today, in addition to their key managers, Scotties has the third brother, Gary, in the business, as well as John's son and Tom's son-in-law. Tom and John both pointed out that most of the successful companies in their industry are family businesses.

CHAPTER 2

Conflict Resolution before Family Revolution

Business environments can be tough. Employees are trying to get ahead, develop their skills, and impress their boss. Most likely they are competing with a coworker for advancement. At the same time, managers and owners are trying to develop and execute successful strategies while also trying to groom their employees. And this whole dance occurs in an environment of aggressive competitors, choosy customers, and margin-squeezed suppliers.

Now imagine that this business is a family business with a mom, dad, son, daughter, son-in-law, and maybe a nephew, all with different skills, life goals, and relationships with each other. No wonder more than 65 percent of all family businesses don't succeed to the next generation. Communication is the key to success for any family business. In this chapter we'll discuss some effective strategies for keeping communication open and dealing with difficult problems.

Effective Family Meetings

In a seminar some years ago, I asked Steve Forbes, editor of *Forbes* magazine and family business icon, his advice for family businesses. His answer was communication. "Those of our family who are involved in the business have a mandatory meeting every three weeks where we all meet for coffee for ninety minutes for the purpose of bringing up any issues anyone might have," he said.

When in doubt, include everyone.

If it works for Forbes, it would probably work for you, too. Family meetings are a great way to improve communication in a family business. Some thought and planning are required for the meetings to be effective, but they can be fun and are invaluable to the success of the business and the family. Here are some tips on the best way to run these meetings.

When in doubt, include everyone. Exclusion can create animosity and suspicion, so you should include all family members involved in the business, regardless of their role or whether they work five hours a week or seventy. You may also want to include spouses. Partners are typically the closest confidants and strongest influencers of the family members working in the business. And you may also want to include those who are not working in the business but are directly related to the owner.

Start by developing a family manual. A family manual is a living document that is put together to define the values and beliefs of the family with regard to the business. The purpose of a family manual is to lay the ground rules for how the meetings will take place, to ensure that everyone gets a chance to be heard, and to ensure that behaviors that impede communication are left outside. The key is for the family members to create the manual from scratch. It cannot be copied from the Internet, and you can't use another family's. Every family manual is unique to each family.

Practice active listening. Many people think "active listening" means paying attention, but that is only part of the definition. The other part is proving that you've understood what has been said. You can do this by paraphrasing back to the speaker what you think you heard and asking them if you understood correctly. Doing this does not mean that you necessarily agree with them, but it does demonstrate that they've been heard, which will help keep the discussion going. Typically, active listening is done in a one-on-one scenario when there is conflict or a misunderstanding, but it could also occur with multiple people. In this case, each party would need to essentially play back what the speaker has said until everyone is at the same level of understanding. This approach does not have to be used all the time, but it should definitely be used when a misunderstanding or direct conflict arises. The Harvard Program on Negotiations includes active listening as a core module.

Hold meetings regularly. Meetings can be held weekly, monthly, quarterly, etc. The important thing is that everyone knows when the next meeting will occur. When meetings are left unscheduled, family members with issues to discuss might think that others want to avoid their topic, and animosity might build toward the person responsible for scheduling the meeting. Either have a regular schedule or have a standing action item to schedule the next meeting before adjourning, and make a point to communicate the date and time of the next meeting to anyone who may have been absent.

Plan the meeting. Be sure to allocate enough time for the meeting, give everyone a chance to put their item on the agenda before the meeting, and leave time for open discussion. By doing this, everyone can be assured of getting a chance to speak and be heard.

Use a facilitator. Family meetings can become awkward if there is a disagreement. Other family members will jump in, or get dragged in, and try to resolve the impasse with good intentions. Unfortunately, disagreements usually result in the feeling that people are taking sides. Moreover, because the designated or default coordinator has some power, suspicion of their true motives can exist. An experienced facilitator who has no vested interest in the outcome can help keep family meetings on track. While Family Business USA specializes in this, there are facilitators available in your local business community.

Incorporate some fun. Meetings are usually held to discuss serious topics, but if every meeting is extremely heavy, people will dread attending. Try to find creative elements to incorporate into the meeting to remind everyone that we should work to live and not live to work. You could begin meetings with each person recounting an interesting encounter since the last meeting. Or ask an amusing question, such as, "What five foods would you want if stranded on an island?" Everyone can answer, or you can simply rotate turns at each meeting. Incorporating some fun into meetings will help everyone relax and enjoy work more, and it will build trust by sharing experiences at a human level, not just a work level.

Resolving Conflicts

Although a family meeting can be a great tool, it should not be considered a cure-all. It is inevitable that problems will arise, and you must be prepared to deal with them in a way that will preserve your relationships without harming the business. Differences of opinion are unavoidable in business. In a corporate business, while you have colleagues, allies, and mentors, in the end you are working only for yourself. But in a family business you are stuck together whether you like it or not. So it is critical to have a system to deal with conflict. If you can't, you will find someone missing from the Thanksgiving dinner table, or, in the worst-case scenario, you'll end up like the Orkin Pest Control family business with sons suing fathers, wives divorcing husbands, and cousins siding against cousins.

> **Dirty Little Secret:** Although a family meeting can be a great tool, they are not a cure-all.

Conflicts with Your Children

A family is a system, which means all the parts are interconnected. If you have four family members—say a mom, dad, son, and daughter—there are twelve possible one-way connections. And as in any system, a change in one area can have an impact on a different area. For example, someone wants to sell out, so somebody else must buy; this can change the business power structure, which can then impact family relations. Maybe someone is getting married. Should soon-to-be spouses sign a prenuptial agreement excluding themselves from any future company ownership? If so, who is going to break the news? Will everyone understand?

At the same time, parents are ideally working together to train their children to become responsible and self-sufficient adults who will ultimately establish a foundation of habits and beliefs that will result in the their long-term happiness. They are doing so—again, ideally—with unconditional love and support. And then there's the fact that parents simply want to enjoy their children. Families are more complicated than they may appear.

A business system, while also complex, is virtually the opposite of a family system. The business exists to achieve a specific purpose, usually to increase shareholder value. Typically, the emotions and well-being of the employees come into consideration only to the extent that doing so improves or doesn't negatively impact the overall objective. This doesn't mean you can't have a wonderful—and profitable— work environment where everyone is happy. But we know that all family members would be *unhappy* if your business went under and they lost their jobs.

What happens when these two systems overlap? The answer depends on the degree to which you allow the family system to enter the business system. If you're in business with your family, you can't deny or ignore that fact. You must put the business first and keep family issues out of your company. One famous line in business is to "make hay while the sun shines." Meaning, when there is a short-lived opportunity to sell a lot of your product or service, you should focus all your attention in that area and get as much as you can, because it will end at some point. Then you can pay attention to your other personal needs. Family business is kind of like this all the time—when you come to work, be prepared to work and do everything you can to drive the business forward. Family discussions or issues, as a rule, should be put aside during work hours.

Parent-child conflicts are generally par for the course in any family business, because a family system is intersecting with a business system. What do you do when your daughter bristles when you ask her to perform some task and the other employees notice? Why is your child having an issue with carrying out the task? It could be for a variety of reasons, and thus the ways to deal with the situation can vary. Maybe there's a problem at home, a business issue, a perception of disrespect, or maybe it is just plain laziness. Let me address a few of these.

The child is having a problem at home: Perhaps he wrecked the family car or got into an argument with you about something unrelated to the business. Whatever the issue, he brought it to work. When you ask him to perform a reasonable task, he bristles because he's harboring resentment for whatever is going on in the family.

Solution: Take your son aside and tell him that he needs to adhere to the expectations of the company at work. As with all employees—family or not—personal issues should not affect job performance. If he has a problem at home, it should be discussed at home.

The parent is having an issue at home: Maybe you are arguing with your spouse, and your daughter has gotten involved in the situation. When you come to work, you're the boss and in a position to make unreasonable requests of your daughter in a show of retaliation.

Solution: Your daughter should take you aside and have the discussion about leaving family issues at home.

The parent truly has an unreasonable request: Maybe you like to give your son the dirty work to make him prove himself. Perhaps when there's a loose issue, you always turn to your son to clean it up rather than give it to the appropriate employee.

Solution: In this situation, your son needs to show some restraint in his reaction and have a discussion with you about the issue.

These were only a few examples. Maybe the bristling has something to do with a particular nonfamily employee, and your son's reaction is to communicate to that employee that he's above the work and above his parent. This points to an issue of entitlement, which is discussed more fully in the next section.

Entitlement: The Family Business Killer

When I read the headline "P. Diddy Buys $360,000 Car for Son's Sixteenth Birthday" I could not help but think: What a way to mess up a kid. But if I had applied this type of thinking to the world of family businesses, I would have thought: There goes that business. After all, a sense of entitlement in a child may be the number-one killer of a family business.

[A] sense of entitlement in a child may be the number-one killer of a family business.

I would define entitlement as an attitude or behavior that you are deserving of respect and privilege beyond your skills, knowledge, and experience. We all know these kinds of people. But really, who cares? You can avoid them or put up with them and get some of the fringe benefits of associating with them. Wouldn't we all like to drive P. Diddy's son's car?

But believing you have the skills to run a business when you don't or thinking you can run the business because your dad did are terrific ways to drive your family business into a brick wall. The marketplace does not care what your name is or how much money you have. The marketplace wants the best product and service for the best price. And if you can do this profitably, then you win. If you don't, you lose, as shown in Figure 2.1.

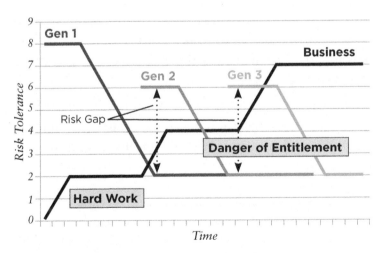

Figure 2.1 Generational Risk Tolerance Gap, Business Impact, and Entitlement

Source: Family Business USA

Entitled family business members can fail to listen to those who *do* have the necessary skills and experience. One business owner's son with a company in the western United States decided to bring all production in-house, over the vehement protests of the seasoned production manager and the CFO. This resulted in higher quality, but there was not enough work to justify the people or the equipment. Because his father was such a natural at business, the son thought he had inherited those abilities too. He was wrong. Today they are out of business.

Entitlement builds up over time. Likewise, the solution is something that must be addressed over time. Raising a child with the appropriate balance of confidence and humility is certainly a challenge. Next time you are faced with a decision but you don't know which choice would be best, ask yourself, "What would a super-entitled person choose?" Then choose the opposite.

Maybe the child was rarely told no, or the parents have overpromised their child's future in the company and the rewards that await him. If the child has been allowed to assume he has special privileges and is above certain tasks, then the people to look at are the parents. While entitlement can come from many different places, the cause and the place where change must begin is typically with the parents.

> **Dirty Little Secret:** Change must begin with the parents.

The Wisconsin National Primate Research Center in Madison conducted a study that showed that the highest correlation to long life is to virtually starve yourself. The reason is that the body finds a way to function extremely efficiently with few resources. Entitlement prevention or the cure follows the same lines. The founding generation started the business typically because they were broke and trying to make ends meet. They went into debt and lived on a shoestring budget until one day they made some money. Unfortunately, once the money came, it was showered on the next generation. The children of the business founders didn't have to suffer like their parents did.

We can all understand why parents would want to protect their children from unnecessary hardships. But doing so is counterproductive. In her book, *Kids, Wealth, and Consequences*, coauthored with Richard Morris, Jayne Pearl writes, "Protecting children from hardships is a huge mistake, because the ups and downs, setbacks and failures are where the parents developed their resilience and the very skills it took to 'fail their way to success.'"[1] Perhaps it is "suffering" that creates the required drive and focus to be successful.

Entitlement can also come from immaturity. If the child doesn't know what the real world is like and has had a fairly comfortable upbringing, he may simply have a misperception of the world. You must explain in no uncertain terms that you are the boss and he is the employee. And when a boss tells him to do something, he should either perform the task or calmly and rationally propose a better course of action. One of the great solutions to this is

---

1 Richard A. Morris and Jayne A. Pearl, *Kids, Wealth, and Consequences: Ensuring a Responsible Financial Future for the Next Generation* (Hoboken, NJ: John Wiley & Sons, 2010).

for the child to go out into the world, to find a job outside the family business.

"Protecting children from hardships is a huge mistake, because the ups and downs, setbacks and failures are where the parents developed their resilience and the very skills it took to 'fail their way to success.'"

In the short term, there's an easy answer that could be effective—firing your child. When I asked Greg Rohde, president of Green Sense, whose two kids have worked for him at various times, what he did when this situation arose, he simply said: "I fired them. In fact, I have fired both of them multiple times now." One of the most terrifying actions a family business owner can take is to fire their child. However, it is also one of the most beneficial to the child in the long run—as long as it is done because the child truly is not fitting in or performing, and there is no animosity, conflict, or "I'll show him" attitude involved.

Conflicts with Your Parents

As the next generation to take over the company, handling disagreements with the current-generation ownership may be one of the most difficult situations you'll face. You're having

Fighting Entitlement with a Dose of Reality

Family businesses have a tendency to create a sense of entitlement in the next generation and shield them from the real world. The kids grow up seeing their parents in a position of power over others and as a source of livelihood for the employees. The misaligned thinking process goes something like this—My dad is powerful. I'm related to my dad; therefore I am powerful. Moreover, typically there is some money, a nice house, a nice car, vacations, and the ability to take off work whenever you'd like. However, the biggest sin is when the parent has a "I don't want my child to go through what I did growing up" mentality. What many family business owners fail to realize is that it may have been that harsh upbringing that gave them the drive to succeed in the first place.

Telling "war stories" over the dinner table or at family gatherings is a great way to pass down lessons learned from even the most embarrassing moments in the family business history. The fact that the family overcame these difficulties puts a heroic spin on the story. One idea may be to halt the telling at the critical arc of the story, and then ask the children how they might have solved the problem. Then reveal what you actually did and how things resolved.

Parents miss many opportunities to teach children about wealth creation; the value, pride, and fun of hard work; and the importance of being frugal no matter how much money you have. For instance, instead of driving home with a shiny new car, why not take the children, ages ten and up, to the dealer so they can experience test driving different cars and sitting down with the dealer while you haggle over the price and terms? It's a great way for

(continued)

them to learn about the process of purchasing a car—including the parents' style of negotiating, and their values about safety, efficiency, and other automotive issues.

My favorite antidote to entitlement is philanthropy. Collect solicitations that come in the mail and sift through them together every few months to vote on which ones most resonate. You can even draw up some criteria such as x percent for global versus local; environmental versus health or specific diseases that have impacted family or friends; animals versus the latest natural disaster, etc. You can show your kids how to use the Internet to research how well each organization is managed, in terms of how much of its funding is actually spent on the cause versus administrative and marketing expenses.

Volunteering at the local soup kitchen, nursing home, or 5K run for various causes is a great way to do good while strengthening family bonds.

an issue with someone who has been in the business longer than you have. They've seen and done more in the industry than you have. Therefore, when they have an opinion about something, they can, and many times do, resort to the simple phrase, "Yeah, we tried that before, and it didn't work."

I had a client whose son was relatively new to the business. However, he was bright, motivated, rational, and had outside work experience with a more sophisticated company. But as he made his way through the business, he periodically had run-ins with his father, and it was driving him crazy. Although his father was out of the loop, he thought he could still sweep in at any moment and apply the business philosophy he previously created and followed. Business is fluid, and once a group is moving in a concerted direction, someone from the outside who does not have the backstory is truly unable to add value. And many times it is too costly to try to catch someone up.

The more common scenario is when the current generation is at the top of their game but is still resistant to the next generation's ideas. When I went to work for IBM, I was in my midtwenties, and in reality, looking back I was probably a snot-nosed kid then. Nonetheless, the professionals I was supporting were insistent: "We want to hear your ideas because it will help us take a fresh look at what we are doing." Indeed, I did a lot of bumping around, trying to adjust from the theoretical world of academia to the practical realm of live global business. However, given license to ask stupid questions about why we did things a certain way added value to many of the business policies and procedures at the time.

Many times, the current generation cannot see what has become of the business or where the business is heading although it is fairly obvious to the younger generation. You've heard the anecdote about boiled frogs: If you put a frog in boiling water, it will jump out. But if you put it in room temperature water and slowly heat it up, the frog will die in the boiling water. The temperature change is so gradual that the frogs don't notice until it's too late. The same can happen with a business, even if there's someone— maybe a son or a daughter—pointing out that the water is heating up. If the current leadership has been around for a long while, they can be prone to dismissing new or different ideas because they have already seen or considered them and determined that because they didn't work before, they can never work.

Another common route to heated discussions is when the current generation is intolerant of mistakes. Even worse is when they don't realize their intolerance. I had a client a while back who was irritated that his employees didn't take more initiative when it came to what appeared to be the obvious that needed to be done. The employees would always come to him for the final answer or approval on any action they wanted to pursue. When I asked him how willing he was to accept mistakes, he realized why no one was making a move without his approval.

> **Dirty Little Secret:** Another common route to heated discussions is when the current generation is intolerant of mistakes.

So here you are, the bright-eyed and bushy-tailed next-generation family member working in the business, wanting to find a way to add value and gain approval. You take an action you think will yield positive results, but unfortunately, it doesn't turn out exactly right—and then you get chewed out. How do you think you will act the next time you see an opportunity? You're not likely to pursue it in order to avoid the possible fallout if the results aren't perfect. It's also likely that you will have some suppressed anger about it.

Another odd, but common, source of conflict is that Mom and Dad don't want to be shown up. It seems childish, but how will they feel if they have said, "No, no, no" to something for years, and then Junior comes along and proves that it was a great idea? Everyone should be happy since progress is being made, but that's not always the case.

At the same time, remember, Mom and Dad may not be interested in leaving the business quite yet. Thus, there is the tricky process of moving them out of the leadership role and into a more functional role while continuing to have them advise on the business. If this is not recognized, there can be resistance to new ideas.

Up to this point, our discussion has revolved around understanding the actions and viewpoints of the current generation that could be counterproductive. But let's not forget that you, as the next generation to take over the business, have an equal, if not larger, role in the process. Consider these questions:

- Are you experienced enough for your ideas to be valid?
- Are you approaching the current generation in a manner that is respectful of the legacy they've built?
- Are you working with the current generation and other key players to formulate a strong plan?

You've heard, "He who lives in a glass house should not throw stones." The point of the saying is to be sure you have your own house in order before becoming too critical of the current generation or adamant that their opinion is wrong and yours right.

When Disagreement Arises

Again, the nature of business is that there are multiple ways to skin the cat, but no one is exactly sure which is the best way. Hence, arguments can ensue when differences of opinions occur. Here are some tips to deal constructively with the current generation when disagreements arise:

- **Have a conversation.** Get an acknowledgment that you would like to add value to the business. Declare that you're not perfect and that not all your thoughts and actions will be perfect. Declare that you understand and respect the current generation's many years of experience. Then declare that with this understanding you would like to be able to express your thoughts and ideas about various aspects of the business—and have them heard. Most importantly, both parties need to agree and acknowledge that sometimes you're going to disagree.

- **Have an approach, and move at a pace that's appropriate to the weight of the issue.** If you want to make a minor price adjustment, discuss it over lunch. If you want to take an action involving tens or hundreds of thousands of dollars, then approach it in multiple stages over multiple meetings.

- **Actively listen.** As mentioned earlier, this means repeating back to the speakers what they said until they are convinced that you fully understand their viewpoint.

- **Do not try to resolve issues once emotions have taken over.** Once adrenaline has found its way into your system, the rational brain virtually shuts down and animalistic defense mechanisms take over. If any one of you is in this state, only damage can occur. Stop and pick it up later.

- **Communicate.** Many times, issues arise simply because neither party is fully aware of what the other person has been involved in. If too much time has gone by without a good one-on-one session about the business, you can run into trouble.

Conflicts with Significant Others

I was surprised recently when, during a presentation to a local Rotary group, I was asked about a family business dynamic that's usually understood but rarely discussed. In seminars where I present case studies, I offer a prize to the person who can figure out this subtle dynamic. Although I did not include a case study in this talk, someone in the audience asked about it. This hidden dynamic is the influence of significant others.

In the family business context, a significant other is someone behind the main person, someone who is not present during discussions who influences the actions and decisions of that person for their own purposes. The audience member asked, "Do you ever encounter situations where people who are not in the family business are influencing decisions of those in the business?" The answer is not only yes, but most of the time. And often it extends beyond influence to virtual control.

I once worked with a family where the up-and-coming son, who said he wanted to run the business, appeared competent but did not convey a strong desire or passion for it. But when the subject turned to philosophy or art, he lit up like a Murano glass chandelier.

Sometime later when I met with his mother, who did not

work in the business, she told me that her son was the right person to take over the company. Interestingly, she attributed all the company's success to her husband's unique personality and then described how her son's personality was, while admirable, virtually the opposite. It became clear that it was *her* dream for her son to take over the company, not her son's. More important, she had been subtly pushing her son and husband to fulfill her dream.

This example demonstrates the potential damage of significant others, where someone on the outside of the family business is driving their own agenda by influencing or manipulating someone working in the family business.

An outside influence can also be a positive; for example, when someone gives advice and input to a family business member to selflessly assist that person with their hopes, dreams, and goals within the family business. We all rely on the thoughts and counsel of family and friends when faced with big decisions, and this is normal, healthy, and good.

It can, of course, become irritating—and potentially destructive—when family members inside the business receive too much input, all with the best of intentions. In this scenario, it might make sense to consider establishing a family council that can put some structure around all the opinions and advice.

What is important is to be able to understand and distinguish between friendly counsel intended to help you move forward and the kind of advice that may be tainted with fulfilling someone else's dream, jealousy, or spite. Always keep your own counsel and decide for yourself what is best for you.

Conflicts Involving Dependency

There is one bad habit that is difficult to break—chemical dependency—which can sometimes find a warm home in family businesses. Chemical dependency is certainly an uncomfortable topic to discuss, but it fits into the realm of concern for a family business—especially because it is an issue for all businesses.

It is estimated that up to 5 percent of the population in the United States may suffer from alcohol dependency and abuse. While alcohol is probably the most popular "chemical" that is abused, there are, of course, many others.

According to A New Direction, a group dedicated to helping recovering alcoholics, alcoholism is defined as "a broad term for problems with alcohol, and is generally used to mean compulsive and uncontrolled consumption of alcoholic beverages, usually to the detriment of the drinker's health, personal relationships, and social standing. It is medically considered a disease."[2] It can be challenging and awkward for many people to distinguish whether someone is a heavy drinker or an alcoholic. We all remember that *Animal House*–type friend in college who would tie one on, get silly, and be the life of the party, but then be one of the first ones up in the morning and ready to go. Although at the time you may have been concerned about him, he is now happily married, with great kids and a good job. (Unfortunately the *Animal House* actor John Belushi was not that way; he died of an accidental drug overdose.)

I know some people who enjoy drinking but decide to abstain for the month of January to give their bodies a rest.

---

2 A New Direction for Men and Women, "What Is Alcoholism?" http://www
  .and4wm.com/a-new-direction-recovery-education/alcohol-addiction-info-
  graphics/what-is-alcoholism/.

Perhaps that is a way for them to "check in" and verify that nothing has gotten ahold of them without their knowledge. The point being that no one knows for a fact what causes true alcoholism. Just because someone drinks a lot does not make that person an alcoholic. But we do know that all alcoholics drink a lot. Some people think there is a possibility that it is genetic; however, this has yet to be proven. Others think there is a correlation between drinking at an early age and alcoholism. Christopher Kennedy Lawford, UN Goodwill Ambassador on Drug Dependence and author of *Recover to Live* (BenBella Books, 2014), recently stated in a CNN interview that drinking at an early age can damage parts of the brain that are still forming, possibly rewiring the brain to crave the substance. This runs somewhat contrary to the thought that allowing kids to drink some at an early age removes part of the mystique, thus possibly minimizing the rampant thrill-seeking binge drinking that kids sometimes inflict upon themselves.

[A]lcoholism and other chemical dependencies are the Trojan horses of the family business.

What we do know is that alcoholism and other chemical dependencies are the Trojan horses of the family business. When someone is working in a company, especially a publicly traded corporation, there is little to no tolerance for alcohol abuse. The risk is simply too great. While the danger may be the same in a family business, consequences can be significant.

The vast majority of family business owners believe that the business will remain family owned in the future. Better said, most want the business to be passed down to the next generation. As such, family business owners can tend to overlook, brush off, or even cover up conduct violations that would incur disciplinary action in another company. At the same time, family members can equally let slide a dependency issue with the family business owner.

I encourage you to muster the courage to have the conversation about a known chemical dependency problem in your family business. Yes, it takes some courage and it will be uncomfortable, but there is a lot of good help out there. And your family and business will be the better for it in the long run.

When to Let a Family Member Go

One of the most difficult family business issues to deal with is the poor performance of a family member. The causes can be many, solutions are few, and failure to address it can create not only an underperforming organization but can also potentially fracture the family.

Entitlement and enablement are the typical culprits. Kids in family businesses grow up seeing their parents leading a group of employees, enjoying some perks in life: nice car, nice office, not having to get their hands dirty, second home on the beach or in the mountains, and having the ability to take off from work when they want. This environment seduces the next generation into thinking they are also entitled to similar privileges.

Parents, in their zeal to bring their children into the business, or by not being honest with themselves, can overlook their children taking too many liberties. Worse, perhaps they are fully aware of the poor performance but believe the family business is the only way their child can make a living. Nonfamily employees can also be enablers, casting a blind eye, fearing intervention is too risky.

Dirty Little Secret: Entitlement and enablement typically lead to poor performance.

Hardworking siblings also suffer. They want to maintain a good relationship with their underperforming sibling and potential future co-owner. They may bring the issue to the parents, who might be torn in trying to treat their children equally.

At one family business I worked with, the kids arrived late, surfed the Internet and slept while in the office, and left early. The father made excuses for them, and since they assumed the business would be theirs one day, they thought they could do whatever they wanted. Ultimately they were unprepared to lead the business or handle the workload as owners.

Family businesses are notorious for retaining loyal but underperforming employees. Frequently the owners of these businesses treat all employees like family members, and overall, this is a good thing. Some of these folks were among the first employees hired, and they remain tenaciously loyal, sometimes even when the business changes hands from one family member to another. However, some tend to lose their ability to add value, are surpassed by others, and have a heavy salary to boot. You know you should let them go or redefine their position, but you feel obligated to keep them on because of all the history.

This is one area where corporations tend to have it easier; leadership changes so frequently that the new leader can more easily, at least from an emotional perspective, let the underperformers go. Once this happens, someone will invariably say, "We should have done that a long time ago." Employees who are family members should not be treated differently, but for many owners, relatives are more delicate to handle. Here are some indicators that members of the next generation are not a good fit to lead:

- They show a lack of initiative, ability, and/or desire.
- They are unable to complete tasks.
- They have an abrasive, confrontational, arrogant, or argumentative communication style with employees and clients.
- Their attitude is overly passive or laid back.
- They show an inability to fully grasp the financial elements of the business.
- They make excuses for their poor performance, blaming obligations and interests outside of work.

As mentioned, corporations many times have it easier when deciding to let employees go because of the fluid change in leadership. Family businesses need to put business first when it comes to business and take actions that are appropriate to running a good business, even when it means dismissing a relative.

[T]ake actions that are appropriate to running a good business, even when it means dismissing a relative.

Steps to Dismissing a Family Member

If you decide to dismiss a family member, how should you proceed? The sooner you address the situation, the better. The longer you wait, the more ingrained the family member's belief will become that poor performance is acceptable, the harder it will be for that person to change, and the more likely it will be that their feelings will be hurt.

When the situation involves parents and children, the first step is to be sure the child's other parent is fully apprised of the situation. You do not want to take action only to come home and have your spouse exclaim, "How can you do this to our child?" Instead, when the child informs the other parent about their dismissal, the spouse's response should be, "Yes, we have been discussing it all along, and we both think this is best for the company and you."

The next step is to lay the groundwork. Perform the same level of due diligence on your children as you would any regular employee. This includes providing training, seeking other areas of the company where they may function more effectively, and conducting performance reviews. Most of all, ensure that their managers are not afraid of providing constructive criticism to all employees, whether they are related to the owner or not. This is harder than you think.

Given that family members may not be fully aware that their performance is lacking, it is important to come prepared: Have a list of instances of which you are aware, add in those that other employees may have reported, and if necessary, conduct an anonymous employee survey. Be prepared for excuses and defensiveness from the family member.

The next step is to identify the root cause of the issue. It typically comes from one of three places:

- lack of skill or knack for the particular job;
- other priorities interfering with performance; or
- lack of interest in the job, and perhaps work in general.

Perhaps your child is tasked to perform a role he is not very good at or he's out of his depth. This can be resolved with more training or trying another job. If this has no effect, find out whether he has competing priorities. (Typically, you already know.) The solution is similar to when there is no motivation—he needs to be pushed and measured to find a way to meet the minimum performance level, or else he needs his responsibilities lowered until he can perform acceptably.

Also, be sure to place the situation in context for your child. Running a company is difficult, and no one should feel ashamed of not attaining the top post. Leading a business is an all-encompassing, round-the-clock job, and the ability to run a company differs from other functional skills, such as sales or accounting. Perhaps your child's greatest contribution is focusing on what he can do best or where he adds the most value.

In one situation I was involved with, the client passed the business to his son, an accomplished sales director. But once the son was at the helm, the company headed south. We were hired and after a few months came to realize that the son was a born salesperson, but unfortunately, a terrible listener. While the dad was truly aging out of the ability to run the company, increasing revenues can solve a lot of problems. We worked to put the son back in sales to "save the day" and brought Dad back to sit in the big seat. The company soon rebounded.

You also can point to the importance of the business's bottom line as a way to address your child's disappointment over not succeeding a parent or not being as good as a sibling. In reality, the company is the family's "goose that laid the golden egg," and its success or failure impacts everyone.

The dramatic next-to-last step is to have this child take a week off unpaid to give him time to consider whether the job, work, and company are for him. Sometimes children return and announce that they've decided it is not a good fit. Sometimes they return with resolve to do better.

After you have given your child every chance to succeed in the business, you owe it to him, the family, and the other employees to let him go if his performance does not improve. Here are some words you can use: *We have tried to find a spot for you here where you can be happy and successful, but it is clear that at this time in your life this work is not a good fit for you. As your boss, I am obligated to let you go. But as your parent, please know that I love you and will do everything I can to help you. My suggestion is that you try to find a vocation that you are truly passionate about. How can I help?*

There will be excuses and even anger. But this is the time for tough love. Don't worry; most times these children find what they were really looking for, or they come back years later with the required vigor, maturity, and focus.

Dismissing a family member is an incredibly difficult task to perform.

Dismissing a family member is an incredibly difficult task to perform. However, if it is done with a clear head, good performance data and feedback, and with good intentions, it can be the right thing to do, and possibly the best thing for the family member.

Emotional Intelligence

We are all familiar with the concept of intelligence quotient (IQ). People with a high IQ are smart and therefore will likely get a good job and be successful in life. However, we have since found this is not necessarily true. It turns out that while IQ is important, it is not enough. You also need emotional intelligence, known as EI or EQ. In general terms, EI measures your ability to "connect" with other people. We know this anecdotally because the majority of Fortune 500 CEOs are self-declared C students.

To be a successful leader of a business requires EI, but to be the leader of a family business, where you have to deal with and manage a spectrum of family members in addition to employees and executives, EI is mandatory.

In 1995, Daniel Goleman came out with a revolutionary book entitled *Emotional Intelligence* (New York: Bantam Books) in which he shared extensive research demonstrating the existence and importance of EI.

Dan Goleman's book discusses the renowned study by George Vaillant (written about in *Adaptation to Life* [Boston: Little, Brown, 1977]) of a batch of Harvard graduates, and another study by Karen Arnold at the University of Illinois on Illinois high school valedictorians, measuring the graduates' success in the workplace many years later. The clear differentiator was emotional intelligence. For family businesses, a high level of emotional intelligence is vital to the success of the enterprise.

My Interview with Dan Goleman, Author of *Emotional Intelligence*

The book *Emotional Intelligence* articulates that IQ alone, while important, is an inadequate indicator of workplace success. Only when combined with awareness of others' feelings, self-awareness, and self-control, the core elements of emotional intelligence, can we predict workplace success.

Henry: When your book *Emotional Intelligence* first came out in 1995, it was considered a groundbreaking concept and has become standard self-help material ever since. How have your thoughts about EI evolved over the past twenty years?

Interestingly, we see that when the behavior has changed there is a corresponding brain change.

Dan: My original book discussed the relationship of the brain on emotions, especially as it pertained to children. "How do we help kids?" was the focus. This has now evolved into "What role does EI play in business?" This is centered on competencies such as empathy, managing emotions, and social skills. These competencies become especially relevant as individuals reach higher levels of management where they are managing others. My new book on leadership addresses these topics.

Henry: What are the emotional intelligence issues in a family business?

Dan: There are inherent dangers with family businesses. In general, with a family business you have the emotions in a business multiplied by the emotions of a family, plus the hyper-privileged environment that can exist within a family business. This combination can lead to issues.

The purpose of a family is not to pay attention to what is effective, while business is completely geared toward what is effective. Along those lines, there is a propensity to promote family members where needed, even though they may not be capable. The remedy for this is to either build the skills required or find them a different position where their skills are applicable. Overall, it is important that family members be aware of the baggage they are bringing into the business: emotional baggage of the family and personal emotional baggage. In being aware, it can be managed.

(continued)

Henry: Has there been any news with regards to EI?

Dan: In a recent interview with *Time*, I expressed that EI has really become oversold. There are folks out there who have made a cottage industry out of conveying the importance of EI and training people in it. What we need to all understand is that while EI is important, it is not everything. Don't forget that there are other things that are also critical to success, like skills, knowledge, and experience.

Henry: Is there a "quick and dirty" method of measuring someone's emotional intelligence?

Dan: No, but the two best ways are to have 360 feedback from those you work with that is candid and confidential, and to use a simulation where you create a work setting and place people in a high-stress environment. The latter method is, of course, difficult to implement.

In an interview process, the best questions will try to elicit a behavior event. For example, "Tell me a time where you did well, and tell me a time where you did poorly." It is the "where you did poorly" answer that is more relevant as it can bring out the degree of the person's self-awareness.

Henry: There are people who do not have good EI skills. Is there a way to increase the emotional intelligence of an adult?

Dan: Yes. The good news is that EI is learned and can be remedied with individual coaching. Perform a diagnostic on what the key problems are, and then choose one to work on at a time. Create a learning plan. It is just like changing a habit. There must, of course, be buy-in from the participant.

CHAPTER 3

Owner's Manual to Prepare the Next Generation

The wonderful thing about family businesses is that we get to work with the people we love the most. We love our children, we nurture them, educate them all in the hope that they will grow up to be self-sufficient, confident, and happy adults. How nice to also be able to work with them. Many times children move away from home in search of work and a career. While you should never give a job to anyone unqualified, it is a nice benefit to have your children close when they work in the family business.

There is a big difference between working with your children and lining up your succession plan with your kids in mind. I believe there are some basic tenets that can be followed to prepare them to take over the family business.

Dirty Little Secret: There is a big difference between working with your children and lining up your succession plan with your kids in mind.

Identify Your Children's Individual Strengths

As the owner, you know how to run your business. In operating it successfully for years, you've had to cope with unforeseen events, take risks, and dodge your fair share of bullets. These experiences are stored in your memory data bank, which you bring to work every day and leverage as you plan for the day, week, month, and year ahead. Moreover, if you're the second or third generation to lead the family business, you also have the information from the earlier generations about running the company.

It is impossible for your son or daughter to think and act exactly like you.

But the way you think is inherently different from a younger person's point of view. It is impossible for your son or daughter to think and act exactly like you. If you're the founder of the business, this may be even more difficult to keep in mind because it took your entrepreneurial spirit, a quality your children may not have, to start the company from scratch.

Interestingly, studies have shown that people we consider to be risk takers are not actually thirsty for risk; they simply have a vision and are optimistic, determined, and resilient in achieving it. The story of almost all start-ups is that they failed the first few times, and then they got it right. These characteristics are vital in starting a business. And as the founder of a successful business, it's natural that you would want the same characteristics in your successor. But you would be mistaken in your desire.

This is certainly not to say that if your children are chips off the old block, they cannot succeed. But managing and growing an ongoing concern requires different skills from those needed to start a business. This is exemplified in one respect by looking at the bifurcated business investment world. On the one hand, there is venture capital, where investments are made in starting a new business around an idea. On the other hand, there is private equity, where investors want to take a preexisting business and grow it exponentially. These are two different investments with two different business dynamics requiring two different skill sets.

Identifying your children's unique strengths first requires you to understand that just because they are not exactly like you doesn't mean they can't do the job. Along these same lines, and equally important, is patience. Let's say you're a financial wizard, and your child has an inclination in this area too. Clearly, you're going to be miles ahead with all your experience. Allow your children to move at a pace that works for them. Avoid showing off that you know more than they do. Be aware that your children will want to do some things on their own. And, most of all, hunt for opportunities to tell your children that they knew something you didn't or that they successfully dealt with something that you didn't know how to handle. If they one-upped you, let them know!

Expose Your Children to All Aspects of the Job

What do you call someone who runs the entire operation? The *general* manager, because he covers every aspect of the business. How do you prepare someone to become a GM? By having that person spend time in each of the key departments. This shouldn't sound like a luxury. Look at yourself. How much of each area do you understand—merchandising, production, management, buying, marketing, financial planning, and the list goes on. Maybe you're not an expert in every area, but you certainly know more than the average employee.

To start preparing your children for the top position, they must spend some time at the bottom. I had a client who was one of the top heating, ventilation, air-conditioning, and plumbing companies in the area. The kids all had great potential, but none had spent any time in the field. After discussing it with the owners, we decided that the kids needed to begin going out with the crews, getting dirty, digging ditches, working with their hands, and understanding the business at the root level. Now they not only understand that part of the business, but also all the employees respect them.

Although not everyone is inclined to be an accountant, sitting behind a desk doing debits and credits will help them understand one core component of the business. Once they've worked through all departments, they will not only understand the specific functions but also be able to see how they fit together. At Olan Mills, our family photography business, my first job was to collect and process film canisters. It was not thrilling work, but I got to interface with every department in the company and demonstrate that I was not above doing the dirty work. The next summer I was moved to the office, processing orders.

> **Dirty Little Secret:** To start preparing your children for the top position, they must spend some time at the bottom.

One family business client I work with has three potential successors. One is an extroverted people person, another is an introverted analytical type, and the third is in the middle and interested in politics. They're already showing proclivities toward what they ultimately should be doing. But five to ten years from now, they'll each be stronger, and the company will be better off, when each person is familiar with every area. When I became involved, we moved each potential successor to jobs that were in line with their skill sets, and then a year later we moved them to the area they feared the most. Fortunately, two of the three just swapped jobs, so they have someone to fall back on. And they are making it.

Now comes the question of education: How much education is enough? It depends on the type of work the company does and the type of work your children would like to do there. However, this is the wrong way to look at education. If your children are really attracted to a particular field—even if it's something other than the family business—they should pursue it, provided that they know there is a job market for that type of work after college. Members of the next generation should feel free to explore professions and not feel committed to work for the family business. But if there is some interest in the family business, your children should take courses that align with the company's mission. If they are really interested in the business, they should take a lot of these types of courses.

Stretch Your Children's Abilities

Graduation from college is possibly the scariest moment of anyone's life. The regularly scheduled program ends, and often there is no predefined plan. Graduates are suddenly basically free to do whatever it is that they would like to do—or to do nothing at all. The first instinct for many graduates—and even parents of graduates—is to come home and work for the family business. Graduates know they can get hired, they likely have some experience with the business, and working for the family business will enable them to avoid the nightmare of having to look for a job. Following this instinct, however, would be a huge mistake.

When young people graduate from college, it is often the first opportunity they have to leave the nest and take flight. Young people should have the opportunity to stretch their wings and find out what they can do and who they are. The psychological term for this process of transformation is "individuation." For most people, their entire life has been defined as an adjunct to their parents. Even at college, while some separation occurs and people do have to manage the basic necessities of life, rather little is usually accomplished in establishing independence.

But once graduation occurs, individuals start becoming who they are going to be, or at least begin exploring it. This cannot occur by tucking back under the wing of their parents and the family business. There will certainly be some trial and error, missteps, and even mistakes. But there will be some successes and small victories as well. This is all as it should be when people are figuring out who they are and where their place is in the world.

Once you and your children have found their niche, the key is to stretch them in that area. Another client of mine has an up-and-coming successor who is ultimately headed to the president's chair. She is still young and looking to earn an MBA with a marketing focus, which is good because marketing is a major element of the business. She has participated in most areas of the operation and heavily in marketing. However, typically marketing doesn't stand alone; it goes along with sales. Currently, she's managing the sales team but has never actually been in sales. After a conversation with the outside president and founders, we will be proposing she leave the cushy surrounds of the home office and take on the assignment of building a sales territory in a different part of the country.

This brings me to another critical element in the grooming of the next generation's strengths: working with another company.

Have Them Work for Another Company

Send them to work somewhere other than the family business. They are young and need to find themselves. They should feel 100 percent free to do whatever they want and work in whatever field they like. That includes relocating to another city, state, or even country. If they are truly intent on joining the family business at some point, they should join a company that has some relation to the business. The son of a prominent family business owner, for example, has been going to work for short stints for other similar industry businesses. This is invaluable experience to learn objectively what someone is good at. On top of this, *Family Business Review* research shows that one of the highest correlations to succession success is the next generation spending some time working outside the business. This holds true because they have become their own people and are no longer just Dad's kids.

When they rejoin the company, it is preferable that they enter where there is an opening that matches their skills. Or the newbie can enter the company near the bottom for a while, until she demonstrates that she understands the basics.

To truly determine the next generation's strengths, find out what they like to do. That's the bottom line. If you can find an area they're passionate about or have some strength in, that's where to head. They will view the business from this perspective, whether it's sales, production, or finances. Building upon this strength requires going broader (with outside experience, even in a different industry) and deeper (by creating stretch goals, encouraging outside training, and working with someone who excels in that area).

Dirty Little Secret: Realize that your children are not you, and your business doesn't require them to be.

Encourage Them to Continue Their Education

While these next-generation members may have been educated in college and had great outside jobs, running a company is complex, so they must always be learning. Encourage your children to attend industry association educational conferences and to read industry and business magazines and books. They should always try to be at the top of their field. This includes being humble, being a good listener, and most of all, volunteering to take or lead projects.

In summary, realize that your children are not you, and your business doesn't require them to be. See that they're well-rounded, and encourage them to gravitate toward what they enjoy and do best. Actively and passively assist them to excel in that area. Most of all, be patient!

Take Advantage of Summer Breaks

Summer is the time of year when kids are out of school for break, graduating from high school, and heading off to college, or graduating from college and preparing to face the real world. These are pivotal moments for all young adults, but especially children of family business owners. How each stage is handled can have a big impact on the likelihood that your business moves to the next generation.

Summer break is a great time to expose your children to the family business. They can come in as regular summer hires, get to know some of the employees, and gain an understanding of the business. More importantly, the children can begin to gauge how interested they might be in the business, and you can begin to evaluate whether or not they are cut out for it.

It is pretty hard to go wrong here. As mentioned in a previous section, one key parameter to success is to expose your children to all aspects of the job. During summer break is a perfect time to bring them in at the bottom, like a summer job for any other kid. Many family business owners go astray by giving their kids more responsibility than they should have or by shielding them from hard work. On the one hand you want to avoid setting them up for failure. On the other hand, you don't want to encourage a sense of entitlement. If you are in construction, have them go out with the crew. If it is a retail business, let them handle the cash register. If it is an office, let them deal with the paperwork. This is the perfect time for them to realize the base elements of the business.

Everyone grows up going to school, but every May it ends, and we get to reflect on our life journey. While we are young we can explore the family business, but we should also explore the world and how we fit in it.

A Mentoring Relationship

Many successful businesspeople and professionals refer to their mentors as being critical to their success in life. It is doubly true in a family business. For the potential family business successor, acquiring the requisite education, training, and experience to take over the business is critical.

However, the best fine-tuning for preparation comes from a good mentoring relationship.

Mentoring is a different animal from simply teaching someone how to do the work. It is more about imparting the "secret sauce" on how to look at and approach the business. The focus is to train the person you're mentoring to read between the lines of the business; think strategically about it; and understand what tricks, shortcuts, and habits can be successful and those that will get you into trouble. Learning the nuances of why things went wrong and what could have been done differently can be vastly more instructive than understanding how everything went like clockwork.

Good mentors can be difficult to find. Clearly they need to have spent enough time in business to share their collection of battles won and lost. Mentors also must possess the frame of mind to communicate their knowledge with the goal of grooming their mentees on strategies to approach business and how to prioritize. It is not an opportunity for them to bend an innocent ear or to extol their virtues.

In a family business, there is a ranking of optimal mentors: those outside your family business but in the industry; outside the family business and out of the industry; inside the family business but not family; and inside the family business and family. Yes, Dad is the worst. This may strike you as odd, but it is simply more difficult for someone who loves you unconditionally to convey hard criticism, and even more difficult for you to hear it. However, sometimes there simply is no choice—maybe your mom or dad is the best at what they do.

If you do end up mentoring your children, the most important thing to remember is that you are not trying to clone yourself. The world and everything in it is evolving. As such, the environment in which your children will be operating will be different and will require decisions and actions that are possibly very different from those you have made. Your children need to be able to take all the knowledge you have imparted, match it to the world they are in, and act accordingly. In addition, people are different. All children have their own strengths to bring to bear on the business.

Having a mentor can be an invaluable experience. Identify someone in your company who would make a good one and ask. Not only will having a mentor provide your children with some business polish, but it will also better prepare them for life.

Mentoring Musts You Need to Succeed

For practical reasons, let's assume you end up mentoring your children in the family business. Before entering into a mentoring relationship, you and the mentee must agree to commit to the process. Each must understand that there is no defined mentoring step-by-step playbook but rather a path that will be followed in an effort to raise the mentee's level of understanding of the business and how to influence it.

The road will be bumpy. Mistakes will be made. Everything will not go as hoped. You can't expect mentees to be the perfect sponge to soak up your words of wisdom in exactly the manner you would like. And mentees can't expect you to feed them information exactly the way they want it, or exactly what they think they need. Be prepared to be patient with your counterpart.

As the mentor, you'll need to let down some of your defenses to convey the most important things the mentees need to know about the business. Gain their agreement to refrain from judging as you go through the process. In business, as in life, most of the important lessons we learn are not from what we do right but from what we did wrong. Admitting mistakes and providing all the requisite details so the mentee can understand the nuances of the errors takes a bit of courage. The way the mentee handles this information can facilitate the process.

In business, as in life, most of the important lessons we learn are not from what we do right but from what we did wrong.

Be supportive of your mentee. We've all been in situations where the only interaction you have with someone is when something is wrong. That's because when everything is going as expected, there's nothing to be said. But in a learning environment, it is critical to provide encouragement along the way, for two reasons:

- Mentees may not be sure whether they are doing a job right or well, and they need to know.

- If the only thing they hear from someone is criticism, they can become discouraged.

Instead of telling your mentees what they are doing wrong, tell them what they should be doing. For example, don't say, "Don't hit the guard rail." Instead try saying, "Stay between the lines." It's still getting the point across but with a glass-half-full approach. Avoid knee-jerk reactions and the urge to compete. You and your mentee both already know that you know how to do the job with ease; demonstrating this is not what the mentoring process is about.

Mentoring is about imparting the secret sauce on how to approach the business, helping the mentees learn how to read between the lines of the business, and showing them the tricks to making the machine run properly. At the beginning of the relationship, it is vital to reinforce thinking and questioning. A good approach to this is the Socratic method (i.e., asking questions): "Tell me what you think about that meeting we just had with the sales department. How could it have gone better?" This type of learning process enables you to get into the nooks and crannies of the discussion and to help the mentee understand the multiple layers of reasoning behind your opinions, as opposed to: "The sales department should have done more of this and less of that."

At the same time, the mentee needs to be comfortable asking "dumb questions." From birth we enter into a learning process. But as we get older we are expected to know things corresponding to our age level. Thus over time people can become fearful of asking questions lest they be embarrassed. This is what mentoring is all about: You are inherently working with someone who knows things you do not. While they will try to impart the knowledge they have, it is a heck of a lot easier if you reveal what you do not know by asking a lot of questions. It is mostly through these questions that the mentor can gauge where the mentee is on the learning spectrum.

As with any interaction in the family business, communication is another fundamental element of a successful mentoring process. There needs to be a continual communication process, whether in person or via email or phone. You also need to focus on listening, to ensure you clearly understand where the mentee's mind is at the moment.

This is a good time to discuss the exposure of your communication. While it may be common knowledge that you are mentoring your son or daughter, there may be other employees in the business who are envious of this special relationship, which is enabling the mentee to gain insider access behind the scenes of the business. As such, while it can be unavoidable to communicate some things in public, there is no reason to do so in a manner that flaunts the special relationship. Maybe some topics are better discussed one-on-one, behind closed doors.

It is also important, as the mentor, to ensure the mentee is receiving input from more than one source. Line up colleagues who are not in your business to share their thoughts about what it takes to be successful in business or at a particular function. Also, conversations and interactions should take place with other employees who have demonstrated success in certain areas of the company.

Remember that your mentees are not you. They have their own strengths that they need to bring to bear on the business. Many businesses succeed, not necessarily because they had the right strategy, but because they simply had a person with a rock star skill in a particular area. If you're a great marketer but your mentee is a math whiz, be sure she has a basic understanding of the products and show her the ropes, but let her leverage her natural ability on pricing, purchasing, accounting, and financing. (And to be safe, you may consider hiring a good marketing specialist to help her out!)

Dealing with Children and Wealth

There is a famous saying, "Shirtsleeves to shirtsleeves in three generations." There are similar sayings in many countries around the world, such as "clogs to clogs" and "rice paddy to rice paddy." Basically these aphorisms mean that one generation starts a business, the next generation makes it a success, and then the third generation wrecks it. How does this happen? Because the third generation becomes disconnected from understanding that hard work is required to run the business. If a business is already well established and money is coming in, it may not seem necessary to put in the same hours that were needed to make the business a success.

Few people could be more attuned to this dynamic than Warren Buffett. As such, he stars in an animated series called *The Secret Millionaires Club*. Reflecting on the saying "The chains of habit are too light to be felt until they're too heavy to be broken," Buffett says, "We're trying to help kids develop healthy habits that will help them their whole life. It's never too early. Whether it's teaching kids the value of a dollar, the difference between needs and wants, or the value of saving, these are all concepts that kids encounter at a very early age, so best to help them to understand it."[1]

One of the great lessons that can be learned within a family business is teaching the next generation the value of work, saving money, and reinvesting that money for the future.

One of the great lessons that can be learned within a family business is teaching the next generation the value of work, saving money, and reinvesting that money for the future. It's much more valuable to teach children how to fish than to give them the fish. Few family businesses perpetuate into the next generation without learning this key lesson. Parents know full well that they are setting the example for their kids by their actions. For family business owners, it counts double. It is so easy to create a more comfortable ride for your children, pick them up after a mistake, or ensure they avoid it in the first place. And it can be alluring to use money to fix their problems, but the most valuable dollar a child will ever get is the one she earned on her own. And the greatest accomplishment comes from trying,

---

1 Aaron Task, "Money 101: Q&A with Warren Buffett," *Yahoo Finance*, April 8, 2013, http://finance.yahoo.com/news/money-101--q-a-with-warren-buffett-140409456.html.

failing, persevering, and succeeding. That is how you break the cycle of shirtsleeves to shirtsleeves in three generations.

> **Dirty Little Secret:** The most valuable dollar a child will ever get is the one she earned on her own.

CHAPTER 4

Money Matters

Some family businesses succeed. Some fizzle out. Others go out with a loud bang. We have all heard of family businesses that didn't make it. Something went wrong—trust broke down, relationships started to fracture, and in the worst case, lawsuits broke out. There are a variety of possible reasons why, but one of the typical reasons is money.

When money is involved, some people's behavior can go sideways. When there is a lot of money involved, some people turn into Mr. Hyde. Sadly, money is a major factor in family business failures, broken families, and unhappy Thanksgivings.

Dirty Little Secret: Money is a major factor in family business failures, broken families, and unhappy Thanksgivings.

One of the best ways to avoid "money questions" is to install appropriate governance. Practicing appropriate governance is the most important action a family business can take. That means having a board of advisors or directors with some members who are not family or friends. Pay should be based on position and contribution. Bringing in a nonfamily leader sometimes is the right answer. There is a difference between being a good owner and being a good manager.

Dealing with Money

To be sure, money can be seductive. Those who work with family businesses know the power money can have in ripping apart a business. Money is certainly beneficial in life, but only to a point. At the bottom end of Maslow's famous hierarchy of needs, money can buy you a lot of food, shelter, and security. But moving up the scale, not only does money become less important, but also it can be a hindrance to developing true love, self-esteem, and self-actualization.

The best action that a family business can take to ensure the longevity of the business is to have a board with some independent representation. Most all highly functioning and multigenerational family businesses have a board with folks on it who are qualified and have no conflict of interest. When issues arise, money or otherwise, a good unbiased opinion can get people back on track.

Compensation is also a tricky area. Many family business owners have a hard time paying their family members actual market value. Gifts and kindhearted parental assistance get mixed up with salary. And then keeping equality among the children gets trickier. If the compensation does not end up out of whack for some members, then it ends up out of alignment in the other direction when all second-generation family members are paid the same, regardless of their role and contribution.

Then, once the parents are gone, the children are left

with an unfair compensation system and the burden of trying to correct it. Try to keep a good relationship with your brother, a lower-level employee, after you've had to cut his pay. It won't be an easy thing to do.

Another mistake parents make is that in order to keep peace among their children, they remain at the helm much longer than they should. This results in poor communication with no one discussing the real issues. Hence, once Mom and Dad are gone, a battle for control ensues. Without the habit of good communication, legal action can result.

What makes matters worse is if the company is making significant profit but there are few other assets outside the business. This forces siblings who might otherwise leave the business to stay in and fight for their "fair share." Having life insurance can help here.

Finally, when there is significant wealth involved, prepare your kids. Teach them to differentiate between wants and needs, the benefits of delayed gratification, and that sometimes the answer is no. Make sure they have had a real job doing real work and understand saving, investing, and the importance of charitable giving—physical and monetary.

The Psychology of Money

Ted Klontz, PhD, specializes in the effects money has on the psyche. At his presentations he asks a few folks to count a stack of one-dollar bills. Afterward he informs them that the mere act of counting money increases the level of oxytocin, the "feel good" hormone, in the body. Conversely, he will stand in front of the audience, whip out a $20 bill, say, "Watch this," and proceed to tear it in half. The audience is always shocked, and some people even gasp. (Note: It's a fake $20.) His point is to demonstrate that people feel physical pain when they see money being destroyed.

Your Family Business Is Not the Family Cash Register

Family businesses face a variety of challenges that "normal" businesses do not have. Clearly the relationships between the family members who are working in the business—and even those who are not—create a different dynamic. One issue in particular is how to manage the money.

When you are in a family business, an inherent level of trust exists. Mom, dad, son, and daughter are all happily working together and individually to drive the business forward. Each has an ownership mentality, thus each is compelled to go the extra mile and look after all aspects of the business.

However, often when all family members have an ownership mentality, they each believe they can use company funds however they see fit—sometimes even for personal benefit.

> **Dirty Little Secret:** When you have an ownership mentality, it's easy to believe that you can use company funds however you see fit.

I knew of a family business consisting of a married couple and their two children. Everyone had corporate credit cards, and the parents also had checkbooks. The daughter was spending money to drive marketing, the son was using funds on manufacturing, and the dad was using the company funds as his own personal piggy bank. The mom saw all this but was too exhausted dealing with her end of the business to put a stop to it all. For a while, the company was doing so well that no one worried about it. Then there was a downturn and general chaos ensued, with lots of yelling and finger pointing.

Maintaining effective financial controls, including strong financial knowledge of family members, is a key tenet to success in a family business. "We manage our finances very tightly," says Sally Crowell, president of Crowell Systems, a software provider to health-care providers. "Our daughter has a background in accounting, and we run everything through her. Moreover, all of our systems come with financial management software for our customers, so we practice what we preach."

It is easy to see how an environment where family members think they are entitled to access the bank account can be problematic. Here are five pointers to stave off problems before they crop up:

- **Have some financial policies.** Who has access to the checkbook? Who has access to cash? How are expenditures recorded? What are the spending limits? What is personal versus business spending?
- **Have a budget.** If you have a larger company, this is not an issue, but many small companies shy away from the idea of a budget because they fear how complicated it can be. But it does not have to be complex. The simplest budget is to take last year's

income statement, look at the percent of revenue spent in each expense category, and if it was a decent year, establish those percentages as targets for the next year. Taking it a step further, if you are aware of any new, big, or unusual expenditures that will need to occur in the coming year, declare them now. Don't wait until the money is needed, or spend it and inform everyone later.

- **Have a financial calendar.** Set specific dates and times on the calendar to conduct formal monthly meetings to review the financial statements, measure your progress, and ensure all are informed.

- **Have a single point of contact to manage the finances.** If you are small enough you can rely on a family member. If not, you will need to bring in someone from the outside. You will cringe at the price tag that goes along with a qualified accountant. But the difference between a good accountant and a bad one is the difference between knowing exactly where you are in the business, proactively driving it and pursuing tax advantages, and basically trying to drive your car with thick mud covering your entire windshield—you can't see, and it is hard to clean up.

- **Have a professional to review things.** Hire a good external CPA who can review your books once a quarter to ensure that everything is in order.

Not having financial policies and procedures established for the family business can lead to poor spending habits, misunderstandings, and lack of trust. But instilling good financial discipline leads to better business performance and a healthy family environment.

Proceed with Caution: Compensation Issues Can Be Sticky

Compensation in the family business is one of the trickiest areas to address: How much should the kids make? How about siblings who take over the business? If Dad is starting to spend less time at work, what should his compensation be? For those who think they are unfairly compensated, how do you bring up the topic without appearing greedy and selfish?

One of the pitfalls in family business lies in compensation. It's deeper than just money. People view salary as a gauge, rightly or wrongly, of not only their worth to a company but also of how successful they are in life. To continue the legacy, business owners often offer more to the second generation than is feasible.

> **Dirty Little Secret:** One of the pitfalls in a family business lies in compensation.

In one family business I know, the son has been plugging away trying to drive the business forward. He has taken over the leadership role, but he does not have any shares in the company. Since the performance of the company, and the industry as a whole, has been under extreme pressure, he has not had a raise in quite some time. And the situation has become awkward: He is now in the position to be able to work elsewhere for substantially more income than he is earning. And since he does not have any equity ownership, if his parents were to die today, he would simply receive his pro rata portion of the estate. (In the meantime, his other siblings work elsewhere and garner much higher wages.)

In another family business, the son is the top administrator, and regardless of evaluations, raises have ended. Most people think he is already at the top of the income bracket for his position. In yet another family business, there are up-and-coming company leaders, but they are still quite young. They are beginning to think they deserve a higher wage.

Unfortunately there is no one answer for compensation within the family business. But there are some rules of thumb: Try to establish an open understanding of how compensation will be handled. Be open about what factors are important in determining the total compensation. Determine as best you can what market value is for each position. This can be acquired through an HR professional, but a rough idea can be found through a salary calculator or contacting friends at similar companies.

Pay employees the appropriate salary for the work they are doing. It is the correct thing to do despite the common tendency to think that the fair thing to do is pay each child working for the business equally. In one family business, the four children each owned 25 percent of the company, and each was paid the same salary. This seemed odd, because they all had different levels of responsibility. Clearly, those in executive positions should be compensated at a higher level than a drafting person or a salesperson. This situation created enormous tension, and it came about because the parents didn't want to deal with the emotions that come from having to explain to one child why he doesn't make as much money as his sibling.

Avoid the temptation to overpay. It sets a bad precedent,

is difficult to reverse, and is impossible to explain to nonfamily employees who may be more deserving. It's easy to see how family businesses can slide into compensation problems if Dad is trying to lure children into the business by overpaying them. It makes sense that if Junior is getting paid more at the family business than elsewhere, he'll stay long enough, and it will eventually grow on him.

Here's the issue: As my professor Bob Bontempo at Columbia Business School told us many years ago, the key to negotiating a salary is your starting salary. Every year, you will get a raise, and with compounded interest over time, you can be making serious money. It all depends on how high you start.

Once you've overpaid the kids to start in the business, years may pass before you realize they're getting paid more than they should. How do you explain that their raise will be lower than they might expect? When the next child comes into the business, you will be forced to treat her the same way you treated her sibling, otherwise you will have some explaining to do. The bottom line: Resist the temptation to buy your kids into the business.

Resist the temptation to buy your kids into the business.

The best answer is to communicate the situation to the children from the beginning:

Son/Daughter, this is a business, and I own it. I would love for you to be a part of it. There are many benefits to owning and running your own business. There are also downsides. At the end of the day, when I pass away, the business will belong to you and your siblings. In the meantime, it's a machine that generates money for the family. We must all ensure that the machine is working well. If you have interest and skill, then you could be a part of the business. However, it's important to understand that it needs to be a professional relationship. The business will pay you what you are worth to the business.

As you become more valuable to the business, it will pay you more. It's possible that one day you may run and own the business, but that's only if you are the best one to run it. You have brothers and sisters. They are welcome to join the business if there's a need, and they have interest and some skill. It's important to understand that all the kids will be paid differently, as any group of employees is paid differently.

They need to understand that because they are your children, they will eventually be owners of the business, whether they join the business or not. If they choose not to be a part of the business, the business will be sold. But if they have an interest in continuing the business, here's their chance.

If there is insufficient cash for appropriate salaries, you can consider providing some equity. Owners can be overly gun-shy about giving equity. As a family business, it is important to understand that minority ownership creates little to no say about the operations of a business. Thus there is no loss of control. However, it does provide a sense of ownership on behalf of the recipient. Moreover, it is an excellent estate planning mechanism.

Now, with all of this said, when the company makes a profit, the owners can retain that profit for their own desires. And as any family would do, parents can give financial gifts to their children. The IRS has an annual exclusion limit for how much gift money can be given before it must be taxed as income. And of course you want to take advantage of tax savings opportunities when they make sense. But it should be made clear to your relatives that this money has nothing to do with being in the business and should not be confused with pay for performance at work.

Finally, as always, the most important part of any family business compensation situation is communication. On an ongoing basis, the best way to handle compensation is to not handle it. Have a high-level manager determine salaries, get the advice of an HR professional, or simply look on one of many salary sites to gauge what an appropriate salary would be. But if you plan to manage it yourself, do it offsite and allow for enough time to talk it through. Don't discuss numbers, but do discuss what each family member thinks is relevant to earning compensation and what is not. Money is always an awkward topic, especially when discussing how much one person should get versus another. But guessing at compensation without an open understanding of what factors contribute to it can create misunderstandings, suspicion, and animosity. An outside facilitator can help.

Negotiating Shareholder Agreements

When it comes to making decisions for your business, the overriding issue is determining who has the most say in answering questions that arise. We generally agree that the person with the most ownership should have the most say, because the majority owner has greater control than the minority shareholders. However, in the case of multiple shareholders with equal share portions, the group needs to come together as a majority to determine control of the company.

Consider putting into place a shareholder agreement. It not only outlines the parameters of operations and the rights of shareholders, but also it includes information on the regulation of the shareholders' relationship, the management of the company, ownership of shares, and the privileges and protection of shareholders. It helps ensure shareholders are treated fairly and their rights are protected. The agreement outlines the fair and legitimate pricing of shares, particularly when sold. It also allows shareholders to decide what outside parties may become future shareholders and provides safeguards for minority positions.

Buy-Sell Agreements

One of the main components to any shareholder agreement is the buy-sell agreement. A buy-sell agreement is a contract between the co-owners of the business to buy or sell their respective interests under certain situations, such as the death or retirement of an owner or simply the desire to cash out. The pricing and payment methodology is also usually spelled out.

Buy-Sell Agreements Can Help
Family Businesses Survive

Operating a business with your brothers, sisters, and/or cousins is one of the most complex arrangements. Indeed, sibling or cousin family businesses can inherently last a long time. As such, just as good fences make good neighbors, good buy-sell agreements make good sibling/cousin family businesses. Think of it as a prenuptial agreement before getting into business together.

The purpose of the buy-sell agreement is to document the details of what will occur if one of the parties dies, becomes disabled, wants to get out of the business, or is forced out of the business. The most common concern is the death of a partner.

If a partner dies without a buy-sell in place, the ownership would pass to either the partner's spouse or heirs. If you think your brother's wife and kids are wonderful people but you don't want to be business partners with them, make sure the ownership passes back to the corporation or to the remaining owners.

But because that ownership may have substantial value, the spouse or heirs should receive their due. The best way to handle this is to have life insurance policies on each member of the buy-sell such that liquidity can be available for the heirs.

At the same time, if the partner's contribution was equal to his share ownership, then the company will be affected by having lost a key employee, which means he will be difficult to replace. Having some additional liquidity to buffer this would also be advisable.

Another key scenario is when one or more partners are minority shareholders because those shares are subject to a minority discount upon sale. Thus, it is important to establish a valuation method for a buy-sell. James Duggan, an attorney who specializes in buy-sell agreements, said there are five ways to do this:

- Agree to a value but adjust annually.
- Agree to a formula to determine value.
- Use a certified appraiser or multiple appraisers and take an average.
- Use value equals insurance proceeds.
- A combination of all of these.

However, from anyone's perspective, it is critical to talk through all the ramifications of ending a business relationship before putting a buy-sell into place, especially when more than one partner is involved. With only two children per generation, there could be at least four members of the family business in the third generation. While there are templates available and standard scenarios exist, each business and business relationship can be different. Be sure you all sit down and have a constructive family business meeting. What you want to avoid most of all is executing a buy-sell and finding out that it does not accurately convey what your original intentions were when it was put into place.

While this may seem straightforward, that's not always the case, and it can get even messier in a family business. With a family business that has been passed down through multiple generations, there can be radically differing interests and backgrounds.

I had a second-generation family business client with three brothers running the business. There was a significant difference of opinion between the oldest brother and the middle brother on the definition of work; the oldest had a more puritan work ethic, while the middle one's view was "bohemian." Needless to say, the middle brother was pushed out. While they are brothers and do love each other, working through the details of what constituted "fair" in terms of a buyout was awkward and uncomfortable.

The older one, the president who was retiring, had fewer financial obligations. The youngest one, eight years his junior, was a diligent worker and married. Once the middle brother departed, the two remaining brothers decided to put an agreement in place to guard against any unforeseen eventualities. And so the shareholder agreement and buy-sell agreement came into play.

Key Questions to Ask

The first reaction in considering a shareholder agreement, which is where the buy-sell agreement resides, is to hire an attorney, but the true first step is to engage in multiple discussions, over time, about what can be referred to as the touchy-feely issues. The parties in the agreement need to understand the personal and professional goals of each family member.

The ultimate goal is that—with a truly comprehensive understanding of each other's situation, whether you agree with it or not—everyone can move forward together. There also needs to be a good comprehension of the intrinsic financial life of the business as it passes from one generation to the next.

Following are some key considerations that always need to be negotiated when it comes to a shareholder agreement or a buy-sell agreement in a family business:

- **Do you need to work at the company to own shares of it?** While this keeps control in the hands of those who know the company best, there may be insufficient liquidity to buy out those who leave.

- **Do you want to be in business with your in-laws?** What if they know nothing about the business? What if they are really good?
- **How do you value the company?** It can be valued by a certified valuation professional at the time of an event, or you can agree on book value for the sake of the business.
- **Where will the money come from for a buyout?** In the case of a death, life insurance will provide. Pre-determine a plan that will not materially damage the company if people decide they want to leave and need the money, which is usually a payout over multiple years.

Remember, the important thing in figuring out how to negotiate a shareholder agreement or a buy-sell agreement is establishing them before you ever need them.

Know When to "Go Pro" with Your Family Business

Perhaps your brother, the company finance guru, has sloppy bookkeeping habits. Or your daughter, in charge of sorting inventory during slow stretches at your retail shop, instead checks Facebook while on the clock. And you can't even remember the last time you all had a team meeting to discuss how business is going. You love all your family members, and you have made it this far, but at some point family businesses must professionalize if they are to survive the long haul.

Think long and hard about how your business came to be. Your family business didn't start as a family business. It began from someone simply trying to generate an income. Perhaps someone experienced a flash of insight into a hot market opportunity. Or maybe someone just stumbled onto something big.

A client of mine declared, "I never thought I would be in business with my kids. I was simply trying to build something that would generate enough money for us all to live on. And then it snowballed." Because they are in the assisted living business—and baby boomers are heading their way en masse—they are sitting pretty. But the founders of this business, as with other successful businesses, had to possess essential traits during their start-up phase:

- a certain level of smarts,
- the willingness and ability to work extremely hard,
- a decent business idea,
- initiative to act on luck that came their way, and
- an ability to take creative and persistent approaches to problem solving.

Hard work, effective firefighting, and a little luck can take you from zero to sixty pretty quickly. But it is not sustainable.

Now let's take that business and fast-forward twenty years. Add on millions of dollars in revenue and a lot more employees. Reactionary management, no matter how adroit, will no longer suffice.

I know one family business that had become a national

brand, with sales across the United States and their own manufacturing facility. But the founders still ran things off the cuff: Meetings were ad hoc, employees were hired and fired on a whim, and financial management meant seeing how much money was in the bank. Showing leadership meant fighting the hottest fire of the day.

Things had to change if the business was to survive. That's because when the next generation becomes involved in the family business, they often adopt the management methods they see. Their response for doing so is typically, "That's the way Dad always did it." However, once the business gets to a certain size, management by the seat of your pants is no longer sufficient. The business must professionalize in order to survive and make it to the next level. The focus must change from working *in* the business to working *on* the business.

Here are some tried-and-true tips to professionalizing your family business:

- Hire only the most qualified people for jobs. This could mean bringing in some nonfamily professionals—one of the major recommendations of a recent PwC Family Business Survey according to Margaret Young, the Private Practice Managing Partner.
- Use formal evaluation systems.
- Base your pay system on market rates for each position. Resist paying high salaries for positions just because family members hold them.
- Conduct regular reviews of your financial data.
- Hold meetings, and take a disciplined approach to them.

- Assemble a board of advisors. Include members who are not involved in your family business.
- Adopt a philosophy of good communication and transparency.

For family businesses to beat the odds against the two-thirds failure rate, it is important to implement these steps and professionalize the business.

Many family businesses fear professionalizing because flexibility may be reduced, the "family feel" might diminish, and it will just not be as much fun. However, gradually implementing elements of professional management over time will reduce chaos, improve accountability, and best of all, improve business results. A better bottom line is always fun.

CHAPTER 5

Creating Family Business Stability

Cameron Evans, a wealth strategist and vice president at First Citizens Bank, starts his conversations with potential clients with this simple question: What would happen to your family, your business, and your wealth if you were to die right in the middle of this sentence? While this may sound harsh, the family business owner or patriarch can only speculate what might happen.

Another method to get at the heart of this issue is to conduct a "fire drill": Schedule a mandatory conference call one morning from home, with no subject, and invite all family members in the business and key managers to participate. Once everyone is gathered, wondering what's going on, you tell them you are perfectly fine, but you want them to spend the day pretending you just had a heart attack and died. Instruct them to react accordingly and be prepared the following morning to discuss what they would do. The following morning, you will probably find that they have more questions than answers.

So what are some steps that you can take now in order to ensure your business continues to operate smoothly even after it loses its leader?

Opening the Discussion

A colleague of mine told me about a family business that experienced a tragedy: The founder and true heart and soul of the business had suddenly died of a heart attack at the age of fifty-three. He had three children, all working in the business, as were their spouses. Mom, however, did not and had not ever worked in the business, but she became the new owner. When the kids came to her looking for instructions, she had none. When asked if Dad had told her what to do if this were to ever happen, she had no answers, at which point the children and spouses all began implementing their individual strategies to influence Mom to enact their idea of the best course of action. You can imagine the family discord that ensued, and you can imagine what happened to the business.

What could have been done? Dad could have taken Mom aside and told her his wishes, were he to die. This is certainly the bare minimum. A better plan would be to call a family meeting, and, at least, he could declare his wishes to everyone. Even better would be to open a discussion so the entire family could weigh in on the preferred action plan.

Enlisting the assistance of a good family business consultant or estate-planning attorney to guide you would certainly be one best course of action. Yes, it will cost money, but these folks specialize in helping people work through situations like this and, more importantly, have seen the successes and failures of other family businesses that are working through these same issues. A good advisor will work with you to understand your wishes and will then gather the key stakeholders together to ensure they are informed as well.

Do Some Estate Planning

According to Stephen Rhudy, an estate planning specialist at Walker, Lambe, Rhudy, Costley & Gill, the absolute
most important part of estate planning is to do some
estate planning. "Procrastination is the deadly sin of
estate planning, as we know that over 70 percent of people who die do not have even a will in place." Many family
businesses can also benefit from the implementation of a
revocable trust.

What about when it comes to preparing the next generation? You may have your eye on a specific family member
to take over your business or simply run an important part
of it. What would happen if that person were unable to
come to work one day due to a tragedy—or if they simply
did not want the job anymore?

One common method is to constantly focus on training and cross-training. It can be tempting to want to
accomplish tasks or run a department on your own. However, what would happen if the heir apparent was simply
out sick for a week with the flu? Do you have sufficiently
trained support to cover while they're out? Maybe you
could consider not just one person who could serve as
backup but a small group that can be put in place to cover.
This clearly cannot substitute for someone if they are gone
for good, but at least there is a safety net in place. And,
as any smart businessperson would cross-train staff over
time to reduce the reliance on certain people in key roles,
cross-training others to understand even the basics can go
a long way.

One common error many family businesses make is to

ignore family members who are not in the business. One of my clients had a situation where the heir apparent son, through a process of soul-searching, had come to the realization that he didn't want to run the company. He wanted to focus on other things in life. While meeting with the business owners' daughter, who was highly successful at a different company in a different city, I asked her opinion about the future of the family business. She declared that she was the best solution to the problem. But her parents never thought to ask her if she was interested in leaving her current job to come back to the family business.

In this case, the job the daughter had was similar to the position the son vacated in the family business. However, this may not be true in your situation. Sometimes family members can come in from completely different areas and be effective, as long as they have the requisite ability and desire to perform.

[F]amily members can come in from completely different areas and be effective, as long as they have the requisite ability and desire to perform.

I'm not saying everything will be fine if you drag your kids into the business, but I am saying that if you have lost a key next-generation family member in the business, don't completely ignore what other family members might bring to the table.

Dealing with Death

Though it is something most of us would rather not think about, death is an issue that cannot be ignored in a family business, especially because of how suddenly it can strike and the breadth of its impact.

In my years of consulting to family businesses I have only experienced death in a family business two times. While neither was a surprise, one did alter the course of the business. It was a second-generation family business with two brothers working together, with the third generation employed and striving to make its mark. Then the mother, cofounder of the business, died. She had put up a good fight against cancer, but at some point it was time to concede, and a few weeks later she passed away.

It was not unexpected. All the affairs were in order, travel plans had been postponed, good-byes had been said, and all had steeled themselves against the oncoming wave of past memories, good and bad, and the emotional sadness that inevitably follows. While all people grieve in their own way, there was an acknowledgment that the family business must go on—at least for a while.

As time wore on, the perspective of the remaining family members subtly began to change. While the two brothers had already assumed full control of the company, there was awareness that now they were truly on their own. They had been trained, the business had been transitioned, and yes, they were now in charge. But the door to the house that had always been open for a hot cup of coffee and a good conversation about whatever was on their mind was no more.

They had a sense that their release valve/security blanket was gone, and they had to assume the top spot in the pecking order previously held by Mom. Two things happened: Each brother asked himself what it was he wanted to do for the rest of his life and questioned how that fit with his role in the business. And they both realized that it was time to prepare for and figure out the succession plan for the next generation.

At the same time, the next generation had become cognizant that the time had arrived for them to step up their leadership role in the business if they were to assume control of it one day. And if not, perhaps they needed to seek their life's ambition outside the family business.

As an advisor to the family business, my role was quite delicate in this situation. No logic, knowledge, or business savvy in the world could have any influence on this emotional situation. Certainly family members must allocate time for the grieving process, and they must slowly ease back into issues that were previously on the front burner. But similar to the perspective change that happens to you when you bring a new life into the world, a perspective change comes about when the one who brought you into the world leaves. The issues that were hot before didn't seem so important anymore.

Death is an unfortunate part of life. We prepare for it emotionally as best we can, but we are still sad when we lose those closest to us. Being part of a family business places an extra burden on us because our livelihood depends on the people we love the most. They are counting on us to protect their legacy.

Solving Family Business Issues Takes Time

I am frequently asked what it is that I do when I try to help family businesses. This is a difficult question to answer because no family or business situation is like another; the players are different, and all family members have their own unique hopes, dreams, and desires. Moreover, the uniqueness of the family, with its unquestioning love, is intermingled with the business, which is trying to make a profit and run efficiently.

My job is really half psychology and half business. So when people ask me how to fix a family business, I often reply that my role can be similar to that of a psychologist treating a patient: I can't necessarily tell you what's wrong, but I can take you through a process to help you figure out what you want to do and how to get there. (Sorry, there is no app available to address your family business issues.)

But let me share one best practice with you. Success in business is pretty simple: Do it better, faster, and cheaper than your competition, and you will win (assuming there is a modicum of market out there). However, this approach does not always work well inside the family business. Sometimes slower is better when you are trying to make certain business changes.

I had a client with a number of equal owners involved. The discussion revolved around the transitioning out of the long-time leader, the process to determine the new leader, and the governance rules that would be used going forward. The meeting took quite some time, and there was a lot of discussion.

I asked awkward and sometimes uncomfortable questions to ensure all the issues got out on the table. In the end everyone came to an agreement on the timing, the process, and the governance structure. There was no yelling, and no punches were thrown; there was just a lot of good, honest discussion.

Later, when I was debriefing with one of the equity owners, he expressed his frustration with the meeting: "I think we could have done the whole thing in fifteen minutes and gotten back to work."

The owner of another family business had a similar attitude. We had covered a lot of material and had done some good work over a few days, but there was an important issue that we had not yet been able to discuss: family compensation.

The owner was a hard-driving businessperson who focused on the details and let the big picture take care of itself. Speed was of the essence; whenever an issue came up, he addressed it immediately and moved on. This perspective paid off in spades for the business over the years. So when he suggested we quickly gather the kids into a room and hammer out the compensation problem in an hour before I left and he was about to go out of town, I demurred.

His kids had been working in the business for quite some time. But the structure of the salaries had gotten out of control. Elements of compensation were ambiguous, and some benefits had been hastily put into place. It was clear that in order to get the entire compensation package for the family members back into some kind of line, there were going to be disagreements. And some people were going to walk away with less than what they originally had.

The better answer was to wait until everyone could

spend the time required to fully discuss the topic, get all the data on the table, state desires and rationales, and forge a solution in which all parties could gain an understanding of what was being done to come away completely satisfied. This is what we did, and the end result was a sensible compensation program that everyone supported.

Business is logic, and family is emotion. When dealing with family on a business topic, especially if it is personal, be sure to allocate sufficient time. If you cut it short, you will end up with a solution that is not supported—and with hurt feelings. How much time should you allot? As much as it takes.

> **Dirty Little Secret:** When dealing with family on a business topic, especially if it is personal, be sure to allocate sufficient time.

Do You Need Help?

As a consultant to family businesses, I am frequently asked, "What is a family business consultant?" The simple answer is that when you need one, you will know it! But allow me to shed more light on the topic. A consultant is brought in to help you solve a particular problem that you don't have the time or expertise to solve yourself. There are basically two kinds of consultants:

- *Expert consultants* give you solutions to particular problems and/or implement those solutions.

- *Process consultants* help you define the problems and assist you in reaching your own conclusion and course of action.

So what should you be looking for in a good consultant? The first and most important factor is straightforward: Can this consultant solve your problem? Here is the five-step litmus test: How much experience does the consultant have solving this type of problem? How broad and deep is this consultant's training? Does the consultant have any actual business experience? Does this person actively demonstrate subject matter expertise and thought leadership? Has this consultant successfully helped other businesses with this problem?

Some people get hung up on understanding the approach or process. I put this as a secondary consideration. Business history is littered with poor implementations of good models. If you can solve my problem, I don't particularly care how you do it.

Two other basic criteria are cost and time. Can you afford it, and if there is a time constraint, can the consultant complete the project on time? No doubt these are important factors, but you should first be sure this consultant can solve your issue. A quick and cheap solution that doesn't solve your problem is ultimately not economical or useful!

Family business consultants are a unique breed because they help clients work through a broad range of intertwined issues, with the consequence of failure being the loss of not only the business but also the love found in family relationships. While the multifaceted issue of succession is foremost, family businesses also have ownership concerns, communication and conflict issues, and ongoing governance needs.

A *quick and cheap solution that doesn't solve your problem is ultimately not economical or useful!*

Moreover, family businesses are incredibly complex entities because they inherently combine three nonrelated elements: a family with a business with ownership. The success factors of each are completely different but must all coexist in harmony.

Thus, there are many skill sets that come into play in assisting a family business, the two critical ones being the ability to deal with the family element and the business element. It is a combination of the expert consultant and the process consultant. Other areas include knowledge of law, tax, insurance, finance, etc.

Just as an attorney must pass the bar or an accountant must become certified, family business consultants must become certified through the global governing body Family Firm Institute (FFI) as Certified Family Business Advisors (CFBA). Running a business is hard, especially these days. Trying to run a profitable business with your family and maintain family harmony is extra difficult. Fortunately there is help available for all of it. Getting help, helps.

Dirty Little Secret: Getting help, helps.

Family business owners have dedicated their lives to successfully running their businesses, but they have not learned the intricacies of family business succession. Bringing in any kind of help inherently stirs up questions that need to be understood so that effort can be put forth in addressing them. Many family business failures are simply due to thinking things are going to happen naturally, or, worse, ducking the issues that need to be addressed. From my conversations with professionals who help family businesses, I would estimate that over 75 percent of family businesses that engaged qualified and experienced help successfully transitioned from one generation to the next.

What If the Next Generation Isn't Ready?

Smart family businesses spend a lot of time and effort to ensure a successful transition to the next generation. Starting early, communicating well, and getting good advice will help with the process. However, what do you do if the age gap between you and the next generation is so wide that the next generation is simply not ready to take on the leadership of your company when the time comes? Worse, what if the need to transition hits suddenly due to health or other reasons, and the next generation is simply not ready?

Hopefully, you would be around for the transition, and preferably from a porch overlooking a lake rather than a hospital bed. But how can a sudden transition best be handled when the next generation may not be ready? Let's look at some strategies.

The main issue here is that there's a gap between when you're willing or able to run the business and when the next generation can pick it up. Two main safety nets that should proactively be put in place for every company, whether a family business or not, are good middle management and incenting key nonfamily executives. Have a strong bench that can step up if needed, and pay your stars what they are worth.

Good Middle Management

Building a strong management team is one of the best strategic planning initiatives any company can undertake. Without strong management, all the power, knowledge, and skill rest with the head of the company. Thus, if the head is gone, nothing is left. Case in point: If you're trying to sell your business, the first thing a buyer will look at, after the financials, is the strength of the management. "Having a strong management team in place that is capable of managing the business going forward, without the president, is one of the top factors in increasing the sale price of any company," says David Boykin, a business sales specialist at Transact Partners International.

Good middle management also provides flexibility in plugging the gap until the next generation is ready. The best alternative is that someone from the company bench could step up and fill the leadership void. However, good middle management candidates need to have certain characteristics: respect for the employees, understanding that the leadership role is not permanent, and to be currently working in a role where they could actively mentor the next generation. This last part is critical because the wrong person could do everything possible not to groom the next generation, or worse, undermine the next generation in an effort to retain the top post.

If you're trying to sell your business, the first thing a buyer will look at, after the financials, is the strength of the management.

If there isn't a good candidate for the top role, the management team could provide a resource to recruit an interim company leader to ensure it continues operating. If the situation requires that the next generation take command, a good management team is valuable in assisting and guiding the new, unseasoned leader.

Bridge the Gap

Unfortunately, although you've just read the benefits of building a strong management team and putting together a good board, many family businesses neglect taking these actions. I point this out because if you do find yourself in an emergency transition, there won't be time to slap together a good board or build a strong management team. The alternative is to hire an interim president.

A good interim president can be difficult to find. There are many folks who tout being interim presidents or CEOs, but finding one who can do the work, is available, and fits your budget makes it challenging.

Incenting Key Nonfamily Executives[1]

The future success of most family businesses depends not only on the family successfully leading the company but also on key nonfamily executives. As the business grows and multiple generations become engaged, a critical issue to the ongoing success of the business is the ability to attract, retain, and reward key nonfamily managers to help grow the business long term.

Here are the key issues that come with incenting key nonfamily executives:

- The family doesn't want stock to be owned by nonfamily members.

- The compensation program for most family businesses is comprised of salary and an annual bonus with no regard for the long-term performance of the business.

- Most family shareholders feel a sense of obligation and desire to share the rewards of the business with key nonfamily executives to the extent they are responsible for its success.

- Some nonfamily managers have prior experience in public companies and would like the opportunity to own stock or receive stock in the business as a form of compensation.

Creating an incentive plan linked to the success of achieving the results of the strategic plan can provide a powerful alignment of interests. Here are some financial incentives:

1 Information by Luther Lockwood, Managing Principal, MBL Advisors, Inc., A McColl Bros. Lockwood Company, www.mbl-advisors.com.

(continued)

- **Enhanced deferred compensation:** Deferred compensation plans allow select executives to allocate a portion of their regular earnings into the plan to accumulate tax deferred, often in self-directed investment accounts.

- **Phantom stock:** The company establishes a plan setting a cash award event at some fixed point in the future and makes book-entry awards to the selected executive(s).

- **Stock appreciation rights:** Unlike phantom stock, whose metric does not necessarily tie to stock price, a stock appreciation right (SAR) by definition is a right granted to an employee to receive a bonus that is tied to appreciation of the company's stock over a set period of time.

- **Stock options:** A stock option is a right to purchase the underlying stock at a designated strike price on or before a specified date. The value is tied directly to the value of a share of company stock, but the recipient will have to pay an exercise price in order to unlock the appreciation.

- **Restricted stock:** Restricted stock grants are actual shares of company stock given to executives that are not transferable until certain conditions have been met, such as time in service, or achievement of some predetermined performance goal.

- **Performance unit plans:** Performance unit plans are similar to phantom stock plans because book-entry awards are made to participating executives upon meeting goals set by the company. These goals are set according to readily measurable executive performance.

- **Restricted Section 162 bonus (bonus life):** Bonus life plans differ from the preceding plans in that the asset does not stay with the company. Typically, a bonus is paid to the executive, and the company takes the payroll deduction.

Overall, the keys to successful incentive plan implementation include:

- selecting the corporate goals to measure and reward,
- selecting who can participate,
- selecting a plan and measuring its impact, and
- communicating the benefits to the participants.

A properly executed long-term incentive plan will enhance the overall value of any family business and serve as a tool to reward and retain key nonfamily executives throughout their career.

Nonetheless, it's the best alternative. A good interim CEO can be invaluable. They typically have seen many industries, have strong experience in all the functions of the business, and can begin adding value from day one. Most importantly, because they are experienced at being a stopgap, they understand, accept, and add value to the reason the company has a temporary leader. For example, they often have exceptional mentoring skills. Mike Carlton, an interim CEO for hire who gained his experience through being the CEO of a midsized bank for many years, puts it this way: "Effective interim CEOs must be able to quickly assess the performance of a company, understand what the key drivers are, and not just work with but develop the potential leaders of the company."

Another viable alternative is to bring in a consultant or a strong general manager. This takes on a little different flavor, because they typically come in and work with the current management as opposed to leading it. For example, I worked with a client who simply had some bad luck finding an appropriate CEO. As such, we decided to put the search on hold and form a management team that included the office manager, the two up-and-coming next-generation leaders, and myself. Together, we are the management team that makes decisions and reports to the owners.

Keep Everyone Informed

Once a course of action has been determined, regardless of the choice, of utmost importance in surviving an emergency transition is communicating to all customers and employees that you are aware of the situation, it is being worked on, and operations will continue.

As with all family businesses, however, there are other factors to consider in addition to the business itself: the ownership and the family. For ownership, the best decision is to place majority control with the future leader of the business. Unfortunately, there is not always one clear leader. Nonetheless, it is still a better answer to have one person be the final decision maker, if possible. More companies fail not because they made the wrong decision but because they either didn't make a decision or made it too late. With 50/50 ownership, decision making can be stifled or even shut down. In any case, be sure to have a well-thought-out and constructed buy-sell agreement in place, so that if either party is unhappy, they can get out.

If you need to be bought out, agreeing upon a practical sale price is complicated. If this is truly an emergency transition, my strong advice is to get some outside counsel to guide the family through the process. Otherwise, there may be no more Thanksgiving dinners together if the negotiations go awry.

As for the family element, it's critical to include family members who don't work at the company. When leadership changes hands, control changes. Ownership and money is involved. Thus, all family members will be interested. Establishing open communication from the beginning will help stave off any sense of suspicion that could arise.

> **Dirty Little Secret:** Establishing open communication from the beginning will help stave off any sense of suspicion that could arise.

Dealing with an early or surprise cessation of leadership in a family business can be a delicate maneuver. If you put too much on the next generation when they're not ready, your business could lose key employees and valued customers—ultimately resulting in the demise of the company. But if you bring in good outside help and heed their advice, your family business could successfully make it through to the other side.

Of course, everyone would prefer to have a clear plan in place to avoid these situations. In the next chapter, I will guide you through how to plan for succession and manage the transition to the next generation.

On Control and Voting Shares

A gigantic area of concern, anxiety, and conflict in a family business is control over the family business. Stock, shares, equity, and ownership all mean the same thing. However, that one thing confers two incredibly important and completely different rights: 1) the right to have some of the profit of the company, and 2) the right to control the actions of the company.

For example, dad died and left the company equally to his two sons and daughter. The three of them each have a third of the ownership. When the company generates profit at the end of the year, each sibling is entitled to a third of that profit. If the company is sold outright, each sibling would receive 33% of the proceeds. Simple enough. However, how much of the profits should be distributed and how much should be held back for growth and operations? And who decides if the company should be sold and if so, for how much? As it stands, whatever two of the three kids decides is what will happen because together, two of them have 66%, which is a majority. Makes sense.

However, let's paint a hypothetical scenario. Let's say that the two sons do not work in the company and really don't generate sufficient income on their own to support their lifestyles. Those dividends from the company can really bridge the gap for them. And let's say that the daughter is a Columbia Business School graduate, is very bright, and has a great deal of experience in the industry.

Moreover, let's say that she has been running the family business so well for the past seven years that it is now generating $30 million in revenue, with $3 million in after-tax profit. The company is well positioned, has a strong brand, and has good growth potential. She'd like to invest and grow, but her brothers want dividends now in order to sustain their lifestyle. In fact, in spite of the protestations of their wiser sister, they would like to sell the business and get more money now.

Given all the years of hard work and sacrifice their dad put in to starting the company, he would now be rolling over in his grave. What could he have done differently? He could have created voting shares and given then to his daughter. This way, his daughter would have full control, but the sons would still have their claim to the profits.

For a company with all common shares, the majority rules (outside of covenants established that require higher percentages for certain decisions, like firing a family member, selling the company, investing more than X dollars, etc.). But for a company with voting shares and common shares, the majority of the voting shares make the decisions, while the common shares retain only their claim on profit. However, even in this, the stress that comes with handing over control would still not be alleviated.

How to Not Create Voting Shares

Let's say that you have some voting shares, and you have passed along some common shares to your kids. So when would you actually hand over your voting shares? If you hand them over to your kids, they could take actions now that affect your retirement. They could sell the company. They could start doing unwise things—gamble, get into drugs, radically increase their own salaries, who knows? Once you've handed over the shares, there is no going back. Or is there?

The point of creating voting shares is to separate the folks who have claims on the profits of the company from those who have the power to make operating decisions on behalf of the company. As such, how many voting shares should you create? A lot? A little? What percentage? Clearly, you need enough shares to ensure a group could split them. For example, if there were three or four people in the leadership team, you would want to ensure enough shares for each to have an equal portion.

However, what you do not want to do is what one of my family business clients had done: create a large portion of voting shares. Voting shares will inherently have a higher individual value than a common share because they have rights to profits and have control. And of course, those with voting shares can also have a number of common shares. However, as your goal is to be able to separate profit claims from control, you should create an insignificant portion of the shares as voting shares. In the instance of my client, as some 30% of the total shares were voting shares, they had a lot of value, which now greatly complicated their ability to separate claims to profit with control, as those with control had significant claims. (When I went back to the attorney, I discovered that he had passed away.) As such, their ability to pass control to the next generation was hindered because significant value came with the control.

WHEN TO PASS VOTING SHARES

Once voting shares have been handed over, there is no going back. Without going into great detail, there is a four-step process:

1. Have a good, well-functioning board. Meet at least once per quarter, review financials, make action plans that are tracked, include outsiders on your board, and make sure you've been doing this successfully for a number of years already.
2. Pass over leadership to the next generation. Appoint the leader, and have the leadership team run the business successfully for a number of years.
3. Over time, discuss that you will pass voting shares and get agreement on who will get what.
4. Pass the voting shares over before you start stepping back, or begin taking chunks of vacation time, or have health issues. You want and need to be around and fully functioning after you pass the voting shares.

PASSING VOTING SHARES—
HAVE YOUR CAKE AND EAT IT TOO

I had a client who faced the kind of dilemma I just described. In that scenario, there were multiple common shareholders, some family members working in the family business, and voting shares that were all held by the 3rd generation president. There was a well-functioning board, chaired by the president, which made all the major decisions. But nonetheless, the ultimate control rested with him. The heir apparent was the "notorious" son-in-law. It turned out he was actually a superb candidate to take over the reins: He was bright, hardworking, and over the span of decades, had demonstrated that he was capable, passionate, and respected by all the employees. He was the perfect choice to receive the voting shares. However, the question was *when*? Should the president wait to pass the voting shares until after he died? If so, he would not truly have been able to retire and relax. At the same time, the president could be hit by the proverbial, ever-lurking bus, which would have resulted in a sense of shock, given such an abrupt shift in control and the sudden absence of not only the president but also the chairman. As well, even if the president had succeeded in making his wishes absolutely clear, there would have been no guarantee about how things would have truly played out after his death.

In this scenario, the president wanted to step back and hand over voting shares now, firmly believing that good leadership required control; he wanted to have the opportunity to still be around as a guiding light during the change—he wanted to hand them over now. Nonetheless, questions arose and persisted: What if having the power somehow went to the son-in-law's head? What if the son-in-law all of a sudden began making poor decisions? What if he completely went off the rails? And although this wouldn't necessarily have been a true concern, what if he were to be hit by a bus after the president handed over the voting shares? It would have been a mess.

There are probably more lawyer jokes than there are lawyers, but the goal of their job is to keep you out of a mess, or at least to help you clean it up once you are in it. Bill McPherson of McPherson, Rocamora concocted a unique way to resolve this dilemma, one that I greatly admire. He created an ingenious legal document that provided for the immediate and real transfer of the voting shares to the son-in-law, with a clause that enabled the current president to claim them back if he so desired. This allowed the president to hand the voting shares over and step back. He could sit on the board and provide input if and when needed. And whenever he would one day pass away, the voting shares would already be where they needed to be. The son-in-law was in charge and moving forward with continuing a great 4th generation family business.

I have recommended this creative solution to many clients, and it may be something for you to consider when handing over control in your family business.

MULTIPLE HOLDERS OF VOTING SHARES

But what if there is more than one person to hold voting shares? Now, you are back in the majority rules scenario, and worse, how can you ensure that the next generation does not waste time with plotting ways to get its hands on more voting shares to gain control? This is where another family business devised a unique way to subvert the subversion.

Imagine three second-generation brothers with a smattering of voting shares among them, one brother functioning as the de facto leader, and all the brothers almost always deciding unanimously. Transition to the third generation would be imminent and again with three next-generation members. How would one hand over the voting shares in this scenario? Who would get how many? If the brothers are all leaders in the company in different capacities, no one person should be able to get complete control. So would they divide by thirds? Majority rules? If one is always on the outside, sell to the highest bidder? It's another mess.

ENTER THE ELECTING
SMALL BUSINESS TRUST OR ESBT

The ESBT is one of only a few trusts that is eligible to be a shareholder of an S corporation. What this means is that a trust can be set up to hold all the voting shares of an S Corp, with the trustees as equal decision makers. The trustees can be replaced and also increased or decreased to certain limits. The beneficiaries would generally be all the shareholders, but as there are only a few shares, the actual value would be relatively small. But what it really accomplishes is ensuring equal rights among those who are trustees, disabling the ability of someone to gain more control than someone else. Yes, as time goes by and family members drop from the business, beneficiaries and family trustees would likely consolidate. But with covenants on how many trustees there must be, the management of the business should continue in strong hands.

Voting Share Gotchas

I was working through some estate planning with a family business client of mine when the topic of financial security came up regarding the founder's wife. While she was profoundly sharp, she had a fairly debilitating disease that impaired her ability to participate in the business. The dad had life insurance, savings were in place, and she would retain some common shares. But as the founder and the wife owned the company together, she inherently had half the voting shares. Even if the dad were to give his shares out, the mom would still have half the voting shares. While there are many instances in which this would be a good thing, in this case, it would not be. Not only did the wife have health issues, but she also knew little of the business.

In this instance, instead of being a check and balance on the business and the next generation, having her now actively control half the voting shares would have been a huge burden to her and the business. Steps were taken to ensure she would be financially secure, but the voting shares would go to the next generation.

Some family businesses set up multiple companies in order to minimize risk, separate land from operating companies, and/or minimize taxes. However, companies with multiple cross-holding entities can be very tricky to manage, especially from a control transition perspective. Take a family business with a married dad and three kids, and companies A, B, and C. Give the three kids equal ownership of company A; have 49% of company B owned by company A, with the rest spread among the dad and the three kids; and have 49% of company C owned by company A, 25% by company B, and the rest by the dad. You might find that when the dad eventually dies, with his estate passing to his wife, she would end up being the one to control almost everything. If this is what was intended all along, then the plan worked great. But if, in the even of her husband's death, she were to just want some peace and financial security, this could wind up being another mess. There is no clear or easy answer to this situation, other than to ensure that you run through all the reasonable scenarios of how ownership might change if someone were to die in the event of multiple companies with cross holdings.

If nothing else, family businesses teach us that you simply cannot legislate everything to ensure peace, harmony, and an effective business. You could write rules and policies all day, attempting to foresee every circumstance, but there would always be a gap somewhere, and if not now, certainly in the next generation. I once had a client who documented their family philosophy into their shareholder agreement and then had all their family members sign it. Though this doesn't offer a perfect solution, I think it's helpful to consider on some level. It went something like this:

> Acme was founded by John Smith and he brought all his children in to the business and trained them to be experts in the business. John Smith was a leader in the field, grew the business, and did the best he could for his family both personally and professionally, for better or worse. The company focus was to be the best it could be in order to serve its customers. It was the hope of John and his children to be able to continue in the business and in so doing, care for the family. To that end, compensation in the company needed to be fair and market-based, reasonable investments and reinvestments were made in the company, dividends were fairly distributed.

To me, this is a useful example to follow because it shows that while the family had created numerous legal documents to try to lock in the future, it also saw the need for a family philosophy in order to ensure the spirit of everyone's intentions.

Spirit of Intentions

Control of the family business is one of the major aspects that determines the success of the business and the harmony of the family. I have attempted to create some scenarios you might face as a family business regarding control, and to provide some potential answers. Legal documents are of course useful and necessary. And good communication among all the stakeholders of those actions will also ensure success. But to double down, consider putting together a paragraph or two about the family philosophy, and use it as a guiding light so that the family's spirit of intentions is known.

On Governance

For family businesses, the implementation of effective governance structures and practices is one of the most important measures an owner can take to help ensure multi-generational survival of the business. While every business needs effective governance to thrive in a highly competitive environment, strong yet flexible governance structures are even more critical to the future success of family-owned businesses, where effective boundaries are required to manage the influence of family dynamics within the business.

Here, I will present the basic forms of family business governance and will go into greater detail about the vital role that an active board of directors can play in ensuring the survival of the business for future generations.

The Three Basic Forms of Family Business Governance

1. **Board of Directors.** Every registered corporation, no matter the size, is legally required to have at least one director and in most states, the number of directors

required for a corporation is directly related to the number of shareholders of the company. Due to its status as a legal entity, the board of directors is tasked with unique responsibilities, primarily including the ongoing oversight of the company's management and representing the interests of the shareholders. Arising from these legal responsibilities, each director on the board owes fiduciary duties to the company, including the duty of loyalty, the duty of attention, and the duty to exercise due care on behalf of the company, and the directors may be exposed to personal liability should they breach any of these duties.

2. **Board of Advisors.** A board of advisors, as the name might indicate, is a small group of advisors convened by either the CEO or the board of directors to offer guidance on a particular topic or on an ongoing basis. Because the board of advisors is not a legal entity, the group lacks the authority to vote on key corporate matters, and accordingly does not share the liability concerns of directors.

3. **Family Council.** The family council serves as the governing body for the family and represents the main link between the family and the business systems. The family council has many important functions, including addressing the emotional needs of the family, articulating and codifying the family's values and visions for the company, providing an opportunity to develop and educate the next generation, coordinating the family's philanthropic activities, and protecting the family's history and legacy. The family council's size can vary, but it should be only composed of family members (both those active and

inactive in the business). It is not a legal entity and typically convenes several times a year.

THE ACTIVE BOARD OF DIRECTORS

Almost all family businesses already have some sort of board in place. This board of directors is empowered with some basic legal requirements outlined above. However, beyond these basic legal requirements, the role of the board of directors in a closely-held family business is entirely what the shareholders want it to be.

An independent director (or sometimes referred to as an outside director) is a director who is not employed by the company and has no familial relation to the ownership. Unlike their publicly-traded counterparts, where there is a requirement that the board must include a certain number of independent directors, no such requirement currently exists for privately-owned corporations. Accordingly, a vast majority of family-owned businesses, especially in the first or second generation, decide to stack their boards with loyal family members who rubber stamp the CEO's proposed strategies and actions. While this might satisfy the legal requirements of a board of directors, filling the board entirely with family members ultimately deprives the corporation of the valuable experience, knowledge, and objectivity offered by independent directors.

If you're an owner of a maturing privately-held corporation, it might be the right time to consider the transition of your current board from a "compliance board," who simply checks off all the legal requirements, to an active board of directors, empowered to provide objective advice and ongoing oversight of the corporate management. This evolution in governance practices can dramatically help to professionalize the decision-making process within your company and increase the odds that your family business will yield the multi-generational success you're seeking.

THE BENEFITS OF BRINGING OUTSIDE DIRECTORS ONTO YOUR BOARD

The decision to evolve your corporate governance practices by implementing an active board of directors can yield a variety of invaluable benefits for your company. Here are just a few of the ways that independent directors can benefit you and your family business:

- **Outside directors can provide expertise and diverse experience to your organization.** Qualified outside directors can bring an abundance of relevant business skills and experience to your company. Selecting directors who can leverage their previous executive or entrepreneurial experience can not only help the management team address current challenges, but can also prevent the recurrence of past mistakes. These experienced directors can also invigorate the company with new perspectives and ideas and often bring with them extensive professional networks that can prove helpful in countless ways.

- **An active board can force greater accountability by the management team.** The most successful CEOs must find ways to hold themselves accountable. The combination of regularly scheduled board meetings, along with the requirement to present financial, strategic, and other reports to the board can help instill greater accountability and discipline among the management team.

- **An effective board of directors/advisors can serve as a sounding board for the CEO.** It can be very lonely at the top. When employees face difficult decisions or want to get a second opinion on a new strategy, they typically have a clear chain of command they can go to for seeking advice. However, most founders and CEOs lack a comparable manager or peer to provide counsel, which can be an isolating experience. While peer groups exist for CEOs to seek advice and share experiences (Vistage is one such association), a board of directors/advisors can serve as an internal sounding board for the CEO, helping to evaluate new ideas and providing valuable and unbiased advice, which can give the CEO increased confidence to proceed with an ambitious new project or reinforce the decision to stay the course.

- **An active board can help provide objectivity and honesty on sensitive and emotional issues.** An effective board can provide the company with something crucial in a family business—unemotional, objective, and honest advice. This objectivity makes the board the ideal governing body to address emotionally charged business issues, especially those where the owners have divergent interests. For example, a family business may be faced with the frequent compensation issue in which the owner's children are being paid far above the market rates for their positions. Due to the familial relationship between the founder and his/her children, it's often incredibly difficult for the owner to enact a new compensation policy that may cap bonuses and benefits. However, an impartial and objective board of directors can make potentially unpopular but necessary policies to help ensure the financial sustainability of the company for generations to come.

- **An empowered board of directors can be highly valuable in the succession planning process.** Because no family business owner is immortal, developing an effective and well-timed succession plan is of paramount importance in ensuring the company's survival for the next generation. For many owners, the decision to exit the company and hand over the reins to the next generation is a difficult one and as a result, the planning for this inevitability is often continually postponed. An effective board can be invaluable in helping the family to plan for the future transition and provide ongoing stability throughout the process in several key ways. First, the board can require the CEO to begin thinking about succession and formulating a plan at an appropriate time. Second, the board can help the CEO evaluate his or her various succession options and help the CEO stick to a strategic process to select the best successor for the future of the company. Third, once a successor is selected, the board can help provide ongoing training, support, and stability as the successor gets on his or her feet as the next leader of the company. Finally, in the event that the current CEO is rendered unable to continue in the role, due to a sudden disability, illness or death, the board can help to prevent a leadership vacuum in the company. During such an emotional time for the family, the board can provide ongoing leadership counsel to the spouse and other owners and can help in the process of selecting an interim CEO.

Implementing an active board with independent directors can represent as an incredibly beneficial step in the evolution of your family business governance. Independent directors, with their experience and objectivity, can bring many strengths to the family enterprise system and their presence reinforces the owners' commitment to corporate stability long into the future.

GETTING STARTED: WHO TO SELECT TO SERVE ON YOUR BOARD AND HOW TO FIND THEM

Once you've made the decision to create an active board with outside directors, the next question you're probably asking yourself is how should I structure this board and whom should I invite to serve on it? Below you'll find some basic guidelines to consider along the way and there is no shortage of publications and materials available that go into much greater detail.

- **Number of Directors:** Besides the legal requirements previously explained in this chapter relating to number of directors required based on the number of shareholders, there isn't a steadfast number of directors required to serve on the board. In general, we recommend keeping the board relatively small to keep it more manageable and ensure that decision-making and communication within the board are efficient. Ideally, the board of directors should not exceed seven directors, with at least three as outside directors.

- **Whom Should I Ask to Join?** First, let's start with whom you *shouldn't* ask to serve on your board. Close friends and advisors already on the payroll (i.e., your corporate attorney, CPA, consultants, etc.) should not be asked to join your board for a variety of reasons. Your close friends, while trustworthy, might lack the necessary objectivity and willingness to hold you accountable on corporate performance issues. Additionally, your lawyer, CPA, and other consultants make poor directors for several reasons: 1) you are already paying them for their advice, so there's no reason to compensate them again to serve on the board; 2) putting these advisors on the board could create an inherent conflict of interest, where they might act out of self-interest and avoid conflict with a valued client by providing input that the client wants to hear.

  So, whom should you consider to serve on your board? While the exact composition of the board will vary greatly by your company's industry, location, and size of the company, current and former CEOs, senior executives, and entrepreneurs who have experience hitting the milestones you're striving for can make valuable additions to your board of directors/advisors. Also, although you should not invite your attorney or CPA, adding retired attorneys and financial professionals can also provide highly beneficial perspectives to the governing process. If your company is facing unique tax issues, a tax attorney or CPA would be a great addition, or if you're considering expansion through the acquisition of other companies, putting a retired M&A attorney on the board would be a wise decision.

- **How can I find qualified director candidates?** For the most part, consider approaching this process as you might approach hiring a key employee. Seek referrals from your network (including your consultants, attorney, close friends, and trusted customers and vendors) or perhaps consider joining an association like the National Association for Corporate Governance (NACD), who maintains a database of potential directors looking for boards to serve on. Another option would be to consider retaining a search firm to help you locate and vet potential directors, but this option can be quite expensive.

How to Make Your Board Effective

Once your board is in place, your work is not over. You've invested your time and money into evolving your corporate governance and the next step is to ensure your board remains effective and provides value to your company. Here are some steps you should take to guarantee that you're getting the most out of your board:

1. **Create thorough expectations and guidelines for your board.** How many times a year will the board convene? How much time do you expect your directors to spend preparing for these meetings? Are there topics the board needs to educate themselves about? The more direction you can provide, and the clearer you make your expectations for the directors, the

easier it will be for the board to live up to those expectations.

2. **Teach them about the business.** There's no way incoming directors will know as much as you do about the business and likely your industry. Invest in getting them up to speed about your corporate history, employees, management team, financials, family values and visions, and current projects so they can provide educated advice moving forward.

3. **Devote adequate time to preparing for board meetings.** Create clear and significant agendas for board meetings and make sure to circulate them well ahead of time. If the agenda includes reviewing corporate financials or evaluating a strategic proposal, make sure the board members receive the relevant reports before the meeting, giving them the opportunity to come to the meeting prepared to discuss the topic and to raise important questions.

4. **Routinely evaluate board performance.** In the same way that an effective board of directors will hold the management accountable, the owners need to hold the board accountable. By conducting annual director self-evaluations, the board chair can ensure individual directors meet the expectations laid out by the owners.

5. **Empower the board.** Last, but not least, make sure the board feels empowered to take meaningful actions on important items. After investing in the creation and ongoing operation of an active board, asking the directors to only "rubber stamp" management's strategy would undermine the most significant benefits of having an independent board of directors.

Give the board important responsibilities and make sure they know their actions are taken seriously and respected by the owners, management, and family.

Creating and maintaining an effective board of directors doesn't happen overnight. It will require an investment of time, patience, and resources to ensure your company is getting the most out of your board. However, for the reasons previously explained, we sincerely believe that implementing an active board is one of the greatest investments you can make in ensuring the longevity of your family enterprise.

This section on governance was provided by Family Business USA associate, Dan Frosh, Esq., Board Member of the Family Firm Institute and expert in family business governance.

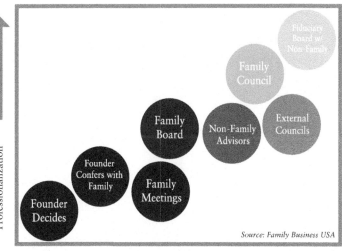

Source: Family Business USA

CHAPTER 6

Choosing and Training a Successor

In July 2013, the people of England and reporters around the world were excitedly awaiting the birth of a rather special baby. On July 22, Prince George of Cambridge was born with a weighty future already on his tiny shoulders. This little prince is in the direct line of succession for the monarchy of Britain, behind his great-grandmother, Queen Elizabeth; his grandfather, Prince Charles; and his father, Prince William. Of course, they have to die first.

This method of installing the next ruler of England has worked, for better or worse, for more than 1,600 years. Inheriting the throne through death may be a fine philosophy for royalty of England, Japan, and Monaco. But for a family business, dying at your desk is not considered a good succession strategy. This type of succession typically spells doom for any family business.

Handing over the reins to your son or daughter and moving into a consulting role while you are still at the top of your game is a far better plan. Ross Perot, a self-made billionaire may have said it best: "There's no better place to live than in your son's shadow."

Where Do I Start?

Once I presented a talk on family dynamics and best business practices to a group of family business representatives at a large industry trade show at Navy Pier in Chicago. One man in his early sixties had a fairly complex family business situation but had not done any succession planning. After hearing about such a broad range of topics, he seemed a little overwhelmed. Thus his question: "Where do I start, and is there a list of questions to ask?"

This is always a concern of the family business leader who really has not started the planning process. In my experience, the best place to begin is to simply declare to the family that you are going to begin.

Call a family meeting, close the door, and tell everyone that the company and the family need to begin thinking and talking about preparing for the future of the business. Yes, you have opened Pandora's box, but better you than someone else, and it's much better opened now rather than later.

A critical piece is to include the family. I met a family business leader at a conference a few years ago, and he explained to me that he had constructed the ideal succession plan for his family business. When I asked him what the other family members thought of the plan, he told me he had not mentioned it to them yet. When I suggested he include them in the process, he said there was no need because he had already come up with the perfect plan. (Perfect, except none of the people it affected had any opportunity to discuss the plan or provide input to it!) I didn't have the opportunity to follow up with him, but I think it is safe to say that he had a rocky road ahead of him.

As to my response in Chicago to the man's query about what questions to ask, I had to resort to the classic Harvard

Business School answer: It depends. The concerns facing a large, poorly performing family business with a number of family members working outside the company are not the same as a smaller, high-growth family business with highly skilled family members working inside the business. One size does not fit all.

To figure out where to begin, dig a little deeper to understand the real issues and to gather input from all the key stakeholders. Armed with this information, you can seek out the useful answers for your particular family business situation.

One of the fundamental places to start is with yourself, the owner/manager of the family business. Many family business leaders, especially when they are founders, seem to have a difficult time relinquishing their power. One reason is that they have so much experience. They have managed the business successfully for many years and have all the connections with suppliers, the allegiance of key employees, and deep relationships with many customers. After so many years at the helm, they almost intuitively know which button to push and string to pull to move the business forward.

Many times family business leaders simply cannot separate psychologically from the business. While the average tenure of a Fortune 500 CEO is about seven years, the average duration of a family business CEO is much longer— not to mention the many years that CEO has spent in the business prior to leading it, and the countless hours sitting around the family dining table talking about it. At some point, leaders of family businesses may lose their own identity separate from the company. The company has become their identity. If they were to step down, who would they be? The thought of leaving could be terrifying.

Jack Welch, the former CEO of GE, may go down as one of the greatest CEOs of all time. However, what secured his legacy was that he successfully passed the leadership to Jeff Immelt. The beauty, however, was not in choosing a capable successor, but in grooming him, transitioning him in, and then getting out of the way. Why should the transition in family business be any different? You have worked hard to build up the business, and it has provided a good living for you, your family, and all your employees. Shouldn't you put forth equal effort to ensure that the business continues to operate effectively after you are gone?

> **Dirty Little Secret:** The beauty lies in grooming and transitioning a successor and then getting out of the way.

The FIAT Family Business

As a consultant, I am on the move quite a bit. Because my clients pay my way, I try to travel as affordably as possible. I always fly coach and rent the cheapest class of automobile available. I flew into Philadelphia one time and went over to Alamo (they have electronic kiosks that will get you on your way in about a minute). In the economy area, instead of the typical crappy boxy American economy cars, I was surprised to find myself standing in front of a little fire-engine-red Italian car.

Most people recall FIAT as meaning "Fix it again Tony" when they left the United States market in 1984. Its true name is Fabbrica Italiana Automobili Torino, and it was founded by Giovanni Agnelli in 1899. Under his guidance the company grew to become the third-largest company in Italy. When his son and heir Edoardo tragically died in a plane accident, the reins moved to Giovanni's grandson, Gianni.

Gianni was known throughout the world as a man's man. He drove fast cars, owned the Italian soccer team Juventus, was considered a playboy, was appointed senator for life, and was named one of the five best-dressed men in the history of the world by *Esquire* magazine. Along the way he grew FIAT into one of the largest auto manufacturers in Europe. With his son Edoardo showing no interest in the family business and ultimately committing suicide, Gianni did not have to search the family bench long to find his nephew, Giovanni.

From the beginning, Giovanni showed interest and promise. He was smart, witty, and had a happy-go-lucky attitude. He attended an American high school. His mother was the heir to Piaggio, the manufacturer of all those little Vespa scooters you see in Italy. As part of the grooming process, he was required to spend some time working on the FIAT factory floor under an assumed name. Later he joined Piaggio, where he quickly worked his way up to chairman before returning to FIAT.

However, the characteristic that probably served him best was his humility. When he was in high school at the McCallie School in Chattanooga, Tennessee, one of his best friends did not even know that he was part of the FIAT family for the first year he knew him. I know, because I was that friend.

Gio, as his friends at school called him, was a great

soccer player, a top student, fun to be around, and gave off no sense of his wealth or future importance. Around graduation time, I remember asking him what he wanted to do after college, and I vividly recall his saying, "I'd like to go out and make some of my own money before I go to work for my family business."

The highest correlation to a successful succession in a family business is the next generation having spent some time working outside the family business. This helps successors gain a sense of independence and an understanding of their place in the world. Gio had already accomplished this at eighteen.

However, Gio did not become the head of FIAT; his cousin, John Elkann, did. John, the grandson of Gianni, also had an incredible upbringing. He speaks Portuguese, French, Italian, and English, has a baccalaureate from France, a master's degree in engineering from Italy, and worked at GE's storied Corporate Audit program. Today he is the chairman of FIAT and chairman and CEO of EXOR, an investment company controlled by the Agnelli family and one of Europe's largest industrial holding investment companies.

Why didn't my friend Gio become the head of FIAT? Tragically, he died of a rare stomach cancer at the age of thirty-three, newly married, with a newborn and his whole life ahead of him. Sometime soon you are going to see a cute little Italian car driving around. When you do, take a moment to remember the Agnelli family business and my friend Giovanni. Then take another moment and ask yourself this question: What are you doing to prepare for the future of your family business?

Threading the Needle

A recent front-page article in the *Wall Street Journal* sadly proclaimed the decline in risk taking among workers and entrepreneurs in the United States: Jobs are added more slowly, less money is put into new ventures, fewer businesses are started, and workers are less inclined to change jobs or move for new opportunities.[1]

This avoidance of risk can also be found among family businesses, where there seems to be a greater reluctance in the next generation to take over the helm of the family business, choosing instead the security of a large corporation. Family business owners who dream of one day passing the business to the next generation certainly must be asking themselves what can be done to combat this mentality. To do so we first need to better understand what is driving this trend.

In a family business, there are multiple pressures on the next generation to take over the business. First is the current owner's desire to see the continuation of his life's work. Many times when a business is sold, it is reconfigured, moved, or simply shut down, all of which are anathemas to the owner. Alternatively, transitioning the business to the next generation can give the owner significant influence to shape the future direction of the company. The message to the next generation that a sale would mean "chopping up the business and only you can save it" can create an uncomfortable position.

The pressure escalates if the family business is a second-generation or later business, because there is a desire to

---

1 Ben Casselman, "Risk-Averse Culture Infects U.S. Workers, Entrepreneurs," *Wall Street Journal*, June 2, 2013, http://www.wsj.com/articles/SB10001424127887324031404578481162903760052.

continue the family legacy. And if this is not enough, the next generation has to walk the sometimes thin line of working for the woman or man who also happens to be Mom or Dad. Finally, the fact of the matter is that sometimes people simply do not want the responsibility of running a company. As Tony Raney of Chapel Hill states in a *Wall Street Journal* article, "I have no desire to show up and be the head of the corporation. I just want to show up and do the job."[2]

Laying the path to a successful family business transition requires a bit of threading the needle. On one hand you don't want to paint an overly rosy picture, because this can create a sense of entitlement, the false perception that running a business is easy and all you need to do is count the money and show up periodically to check on things. On the other hand, demonstrating how difficult it is to deal with the business and how much stress it creates will probably not result in your kids lining up to fill out a job application.

Practice and actual experience are some of the most important aspects of bringing the next generation along. Give them summer jobs while they are in high school and college where they can learn the various aspects of the business. Allow them as much responsibility as they would like to have, but don't force them to overreach their abilities. As they progress, and when they join the family business full time, find some group initiatives. This will expose them to actually working in a group and seeing group dynamics. This is the first step to developing people and leadership skills. At the same time, give them some individual projects where they are solely responsible for the results.

---

2 Ibid.

This generates a sense of ownership and helps them learn to reach out to others for information and help. The bottom line: Move them up the ladder as fast as they are willing and able to go, while exposing them to the next rung just out of reach.

> **Dirty Little Secret:** Laying the path to a successful family business transition requires a bit of threading the needle.

Finally, be honest. State the opportunity early, but paint it accurately. Yes, it can be stressful, but with better training and preparation than you had, it can be manageable and generate a rewarding life.

Tips for How to Select the Next Family Business Leader

So who will lead the family business in the next generation? This is the most vexing question facing any family business owner contemplating the succession task.

With the birth rate still around 2.2 children per couple, and cousins and in-laws added to the mix, the typical family business could have multiple family members in the next generation vying for position as the future leader. Moreover, it is highly likely that one or more high-performing employees could be, or want to be, considered to take the helm of the company.

The first default position is to not make a decision. There are a variety of ways to do this:

- **Divide the company into parts and let each sibling run that portion.** Unfortunately, it is rare that a company has the size to split up, and even if it does, this would negatively impact efficiencies. More common would be heading up different divisions. However, this still leaves company-wide decisions as shared responsibility.
- **Rotate the leadership role.** Every six or twelve months each sibling takes a turn running the company. This sounds good in theory but undermines strategy implementation, consistent leadership style, and having one face to the customer.
- **Share the leadership role.** This is the default situation when no leader is chosen. There are many family businesses that manage to run the leadership of the company as a committee. But there are more that fail. The trick is to have a strong culture of respectful communication and to truly understand and be okay with the fact that sometimes your idea, despite your passion for it, may need to be given up.
- **Buy another business to allow one of the siblings to run that.** Again, not all family businesses have the wherewithal to run out and purchase another business. A better and more practical derivation of this is to fund the start-up of another business. However, this needs to be done in a professional manner with the intention and belief that it can be successful, not just to give possible successors something to do to keep occupied or keep them out of the business.

- **Bring in or select a nonfamily member to lead the company.** There are two ways this can be done: the right way and the wrong way. The right way is to have a truly qualified professional who is respected in the industry and by the family members to lead the company. The wrong way is to put someone in place who is called the leader but whose job is really to negotiate between the siblings.

If you truly would like to increase the chances of the family business continuing successfully into the future, choose a leader. As such, the importance of leadership must be discussed and understood. Libraries of books are written on its importance, and myriad historical examples exist on which to reflect. And we read every day about the impact CEOs, entrepreneurs, and coaches have on their teams. Equally important, explain to your children that they are loved for who they are, and just because one may be chosen as the leader, it has no bearing on the love you as parents feel for each child. If the company does well, everyone does well.

> **Dirty Little Secret:** If the company does well, everyone does well.

So how do you choose? The best method is to create or obtain a job description for the leader of a company like yours in your industry. While this can be done through interviews, research, and your own experience, bringing in an outside HR professional will create great credibility and impartiality. Once this is established, bringing in outside business professionals to complement the evaluation process can be invaluable. The ideal situation is to have a board of advisors in place to coordinate this effort.

The final critical element in selecting the next leader to run the family business is to realize that it is not all about who will lead. It is also about ensuring that those relatives who are not selected will support the decision and can work as a team with the new leader. And remember, maybe the best leader is not one of the family members at all.

Contributions of a Nonfamily CEO

As CEO of a 125-year-old family company, I reported to the fourth-generation chairman. I was not the first nonfamily member in that position, but my few predecessors had grown up with the chairman. I had been hired from the outside, and after a dozen years in preparation I was still to be tested. To succeed I had several essential elements in my favor.

I was an important link between generations. The next generation was in middle management, and I could offer the opportunities they needed to achieve their destinies. A prerequisite was running the business well, with particular attention to their growth.

Adding to my good fortune, after his long and highly successful tenure as company head, the chairman was ready to delegate the business to me and my strong group of senior managers. He was hardly bashful about offering new ideas and critiques, but I was the CEO. How often is the founder and owner of a company capable of giving rein to an appointed head? Note Nike, Starbucks, and so many others in which intentions to step aside crumble upon the first whiff of not doing it "my way."

Not that I forgot who owned the place. One morning the chairman appeared in my office to ask a favor. "I know you are against this capital expenditure, but I want it, and if you will propose it to the board I won't ask you for it again." [His request] made my day, but that night I realized that if he wanted [to do so] again, he'd find another to say yes.

Underlying this situation, the chairman and I shared the core human values that led to our being annually named as one of the 100 Best Companies to work for. The two of us were distant socially and in status, but these shared beliefs created compatibility and credibility.

There were downsides. I had no status in the business world. Successes were family successes. A tough part of my job as a nonfamily CEO in a family company was making organizational choices that had a business purpose but were also timed to the career progression of the next generation. Communications between us were sometimes uncomfortable, but it was important for me to be the positive link between the family and the organization. Later, my successor phoned to say he had no idea how much time I had spent in the chairman's office.

Several years into retirement I take great satisfaction from my contribution to one of the most successful family enterprises of all time.

Bill George

Former CEO of SC Johnson

At the Right Times, Less Leadership Can Be More

If you are the current generation leading a family business, you might be asking yourself: How do I lead us through this process? or something along those lines. As the leader of the family business, it is your responsibility to chart a course for a successful transition that covers changes in ownership and leadership, addresses estate planning and wealth preservation, and maintains family harmony along the way. While this is sufficiently overwhelming by itself, I'd like to focus on what may be the most difficult part of succession for the current generation.

At first it didn't compute for me that Jerry Yang, the cofounder of Yahoo, "resigned" from the board of directors of his own company. He was only forty-three; he had a great company; it was the only thing he knew; and heck, he was the founder! Did he really have that much of a hankering to hit the golf course every day? Of course not—he was fired. Perhaps more delicately worded, he was shown the light.

The number-one succession issue facing a family business is the inability of the current leader to make space for the next generation. Part of the problem is that it is so counterintuitive: The way to lead the family business through succession is to *stop leading.* Jeff Krepps, a family systems specialist, describes it this way: "When a child leaves home, parenting must also change. Otherwise the relationship can break down. This dynamic is also present in family business succession, but instead of the parent reacting to the change, they must proactively change their behavior." They need to step back a bit.

Yes, it is incredibly difficult to do. You are the expert at what you do—you anticipate issues and opportunities before they exist; and have deep bonds with customers, suppliers, and employees through years of battle in the marketplace. But now I ask you, what would happen to your family business if you went on vacation for a month with no phone or email? Or if you got hit by the proverbial truck?

There are some obstacles to letting go. First, after so many years, you are good at what you do, you know most of the answers immediately, and you don't want to hand over decisions where mistakes can be made. But we know that for people to learn something, they must do it themselves and make some mistakes. (My wife and I are trying to teach our kids to cook, so we accept that some pans will get ruined.)

> **Dirty Little Secret:** There are some obstacles to letting go.

The second issue is that the next generation will want to change the business in some way. You are not going to like these ideas because you have either tried them before and don't think they will work, or you lack confidence in the next generation to execute. However, you may want to also consider that you are probably a little more risk averse than you used to be. Family businesses that have grown from one generation to the next didn't achieve the growth because they sat on the business they were handed. They made some changes. It's far better that the next generation tries new ideas while you are ready and able to help.

But perhaps, as discussed earlier, the biggest obstacle is that you have become synonymous with the business. People identify you as the company. Thus, relinquishing some control or responsibility of the company begs the question: Who am I if I am not leading this company? This can be a scary thought.

Creating some space for the next generation to step up is not always easy or comfortable. If the company is doing well, why rock the boat? If the company is doing poorly, while you may have a lot to offer, perhaps you are standing in the way of progress. Maybe this is what someone at Yahoo helped Jerry Yang figure out.

Show Them You've Got What It Takes to Take Over the Business

Perhaps you are a next-generation family member thinking about the future of your family's business. Perhaps you have enjoyed your work in the company so far. You got a bird's-eye view into the real operational issues of the business at an early age and privileged access to upper management (a.k.a. Mom and Dad), and the top management team listens to you. As the next generation working in the business, it would certainly seem that if you stick around, one day this could all be yours. Well, maybe.

It is important for successors to understand that when the current leadership steps down, they're going to want to get some value from the business they've worked so hard to build. There are a variety of options out there: They could sell to a competitor, bring in private equity partners, or sell to an internal group of nonfamily managers. For certain companies, setting up an employee stock ownership plan (ESOP) could be another option.

If you are interested in taking over your family company, you need to demonstrate that you are indeed the best alternative. To start, you must have a good sense of who you are and what your values are and be able to stand behind those values. This means you can remain calm in an environment of disagreement, conflict, rejection, and even personal attacks, and think through situations rationally instead of emotionally. You take action and make decisions based on careful thinking and internal beliefs without reacting to pressure from others. You don't succumb to others in seeking approval or force others to your beliefs. What is core here are your independence and the principles you stand behind.

Working in a family business can make it difficult to develop a sense of independence. Since you were born, Mom and Dad have been telling you how you should live your life, and now that you are an employee, they're telling you how to run the business. Clearly, we all must go through the learning stage, which inherently means you're dependent on the teacher. But at some point, you must assert yourself as capable of operating some or all parts of the business without relying on your parents.

Carry the correct expectations: Don't seek or expect special treatment because you are a family member. Employees outside your family expect you to receive special treatment—prove them wrong. Start at the bottom, and earn your way up. Come in early, stay late, and take on those tasks that need to be done but no one wants to do. You'll gain more respect and cooperation down the road if everyone knows you've dug the ditches—and will dig the ditch right now if needed.

Competence is twofold: It entails being reliable and dependable, and being able to perform required tasks well. Regardless of the job, you must arrive at work on time, dressed and groomed appropriately. You must be honest and diligent in your work; meet deadlines; and show respect and courtesy to employees, customers, and vendors. At the same time, you must perform your job well and strive to become the best you can be in your role, whether it's in sales, purchasing, or customer service.

Seek out feedback from others on how you're doing and advice on how you can improve. Move around to other departments, too, if you can. If you've been in accounting for some time, try moving to marketing. Attend the industry conferences and lead some of the sessions. Read the industry magazines to take in as much information as you can. Practice continual personal development (CPD).

Become a good communicator. This does not mean talking all the time but rather establishing an environment where people know they can talk to you about issues, and that you, in turn, keep others informed about your actions and intentions. Others should consider you a good listener. Practice active listening by paraphrasing back to speakers what they said. Hold or actively participate in meetings, and be inclusive in meetings and conversations.

Once you have established your independence and demonstrated your competence, raise your level of participation in and perspective of the business outside of the functional areas to a more strategic level: Where should we be going with this business? How should we react to competition? How do we prepare to become a better company in the future? Always ask yourself: What actions can we take to double revenue?

While each of these areas has an entire college course to support them, these guidelines represent a tried-and-true path to a successful family business succession to the next generation. When the time comes for Mom and Dad to retire, make it a foregone conclusion that you should be the one to take the company into the future.

Plan Now for Selling the Family Business Later

Maybe you're an aging business owner with an eye on retirement. Or you're an entrepreneur who has been ready to sell the family business for a while, but you were waiting for signs of an improving economy. In any case, you are considering selling the family business—perhaps now, perhaps a few years from now. What should you do now to get ready?

You've already accomplished much by thinking along these lines, according to experts. You have been able to overcome the idea of parting from the business, and you are willing to sell to someone outside the family.

"This might actually be the hardest part of the entire process," says Walter Zweifler, a New York–based financial researcher who has been appraising privately held businesses since 1976 and has consulted with many family business owners who have considered selling. "Business owners do not think they will ever die and have enormous trouble psychologically coming to grips with not owning or running the business."

Now that you've gotten past that part, here are other things you should be thinking about to get ready:

- End the family perks. That means no more sports tickets, toys with motors, or nonworking family members on the payroll.
- Show some profits. Demonstrating strong earnings attracts buyers.
- Get inventory straight, accurate, and current.
- Have an outside party audit your financials so the buyer can trust them.
- Strengthen management. Show that the business can operate without you.
- Get outside help in selling your business. Even lawyers don't represent themselves. If you're a small company, find a business broker through your local chamber of commerce. If you're a larger company, go to a qualified investment banking firm for help finding a certified professional experienced in buying and selling businesses on behalf of people.

Once you have found an interested party, realize buyers and sellers may still have to negotiate to optimize the deal for both sides. For example, perhaps the seller wants to stay on for the next couple of years, but the buyer is ready to buy today. A possible answer to this is that the seller can reduce the price of the company in exchange for staying on under a three-year salaried contract. That way, the seller is happy, and the buyer doesn't have to pay as much up front.

It is every business owner's dream to see their life's work

continue and grow within the family. But maybe, if you are honest with yourself and can overcome the emotional barriers, you will see that the intelligent prep and sale of the business will enable you to leave a financial legacy that will benefit your family for many generations to come.

Will Your Successor Be Ready to Lead Well?

Succession in the family business is undoubtedly the foundational issue of family business dynamics. But when we say succession, do we mean ownership, leadership, estate planning, or "What the heck will I do with myself if I am not running this place?"

Once I attended a client's holiday party. It was a nice affair with good employee representation. As is protocol, the owner and founder stood up to thank all the staff for their hard work during the year and then took a moment to recount the sixty-year history of the company. And in closing he made one final announcement: Effective immediately his son would be the president of the company.

What do you think the reaction of the employees was? What do you think it would be for most family businesses? Could be good, bad, or ugly. Chances are this declaration would not evoke a unanimously positive response. But in this case there was widespread and sincere applause, cheering, and standing ovations. Why did this passing of the baton happen so smoothly? Because the next generation was ready.

Yes, there are many questions that need to be answered

to have a successful family business transition. But lining up the next generation of business leadership is at the core. Following are some key ingredients to developing a successful next-generation family business leader:

- **Independence:** Next-generation leaders must have confidence in themselves, their thoughts, and their beliefs. Much of this can be developed while working in the family business by constructing and leading significant projects. In the case of my client, he began a division, got a loan, hired employees, and increased revenues more than 15 percent. But the shortcut to creating the required mentality is to work somewhere else early on. This is why so many multigenerational family businesses include this requirement in their family business constitution.

- **Competence:** This is more than just being able to do the work. It means developing bottom-up experience. Not only being the accountant but also being able to reconcile the accounts and perform the journal entries. Not only being a sales and marketing manager but also having been on quota and worked the trade shows. IBM, originally a family business, had an unwritten rule that to be a top executive you needed to have spent time working as a sales representative. It also required that you gain some level of external knowledge and training regarding your function, whether through reading relevant material or attending seminars and workshops.

- **An ability to work well with people:** It is not enough simply to be smart and confident. You need to be able to work with people. The book *Emotional*

Intelligence by Daniel Goleman outlines two studies measuring the success of a batch of high school
valedictorians and Harvard graduates. He found that
those who possessed the ability to perceive the emotional state of others and react to it in an appropriate
manner were much more successful in their careers.
The ability to effectively communicate falls into this
same category.

- **No special privileges:** Showing up to work on time,
  staying late, taking on special projects, and being
  measured by the same metrics as everyone else shows
  that you are part of the team and that you want
  to be judged on the merits of your work, not your
  bloodline. This will help the next generation gain the
  respect of coworkers.

Stepping back, these qualities could simply be labeled
leadership. Steve Miller, cofounder of the University of
North Carolina Family Enterprise Center, encapsulates it
this way: "There are many factors attributable to the success of a family business, but none is more essential than
leadership. The difference between those family businesses
that succeed and those that flounder or fail can many times
be chalked up to the quality of leadership."

In the next chapter, I'll discuss how you can make this
transition smooth and be confident that you are leaving
your business in good hands.

CHAPTER 7

When Family Isn't the Right Fit for the Future

The dream of most family business owners is to hand the business over to their children with the hope that it will continue for many generations to come. My goal is to try to help them achieve that dream, if possible. Unfortunately, some family businesses simply should not go to the next generation. Yes, it can be sad, but trying to force a square peg into a round hole will only create a great deal of damage. Relationships will become frayed, wealth can be negatively impacted, and lives can be wasted.

[S]ome family businesses simply should not go to the next generation.

When the default plan changes, business owners often experience much consternation over figuring out a succession plan. However, this does not have to be the case. The fact is that many family businesses are not designed to be passed down to the next generation.

If you are running a small retail store and it does well enough to pay for your kids to receive a top-notch education, then most likely your kids will not aspire to come back and run the family business. At the same time, many first-generation businesses can be in a field dependent on fast-moving technology or significant creativity. For these businesses, it is difficult to find anyone who can lead the company, making it unlikely the next generation will possess the required rare skills or natural ability. I had a client that fell into this last category.

The founder of the company has an engineering degree from a prestigious university and worked as a senior engineer at Rockwell International for many years. He now runs his own company providing custom engineering solutions. While his children are bright and motivated, none have an engineering background. Given the highly technical and ever-changing nature of the products and services, it is unlikely the next generation will be able to lead the company in the future.

Then there are financial constraints. Consider an owner whose total net worth is almost entirely in the family business. One child is in the business and three are not. Can a parent reasonably leave the entire estate to only one child? Not likely. And if the other siblings do become shared owners, the pressure on the one running the business can be so unbearable that he or she may jump at the chance to sell it.

Another financial scenario is when the number of owners in a multigenerational family business has simply outgrown the ability of the company to provide the jobs or size of dividends desired by the many family owners, forcing the question of selling the business.

However, the most obvious reason many family businesses do not pass from one generation to the next is simply that the next generation has chosen a different career path.

If the company is an engineering company and the daughter has her master's degree in psychology, then she is probably not a good fit.

All these "natural events" whittle down the number of family businesses that need to work on figuring out succession. The "unnatural events" are, of course, when your kids are clearly not capable or interested, or are so passionate and skilled they have already taken over and grown the business beyond what you thought possible.

Clear away all of this and you are left with quite a few family businesses that truly need to put forth effort figuring out and working through a succession plan. And to this end, it is important for these family business owners to understand the overall objective of succession: Preserve the wealth that has been built up through the business, and retain harmony among all family members.

Dirty Little Secret: Preserve the wealth that has been built up through the business, and retain harmony among all family members.

If the wealth of the business erodes, no one will be happy. But if the wealth is retained and family relationships are damaged, that is not success either. Many times we fixate on the wealth aspect, but let us remind ourselves of the importance of upholding family relationships.

Family Businesses and Family Must Sometimes Part Ways

I am often asked what is more important in a family business: the family or the business? My first instinct is to explain that this is not the proper question because it assumes that you can only have success in one area and not both. While sometimes difficult to achieve, you can have family harmony *and* a successful business.

This question often arises when the family squabbles have become so intense or so intractable that someone declares, "We should all throw in the towel and sell the business." Sometimes it comes simply because there is no more energy to deal with the issues.

I had a client who would regularly threaten to sell the business when he was not having a good day, people were not responding to his bad ideas, or he was simply not being shown the respect he thought he deserved.

He could not see that he was the problem. The company had grown beyond his capabilities. Because they could not get him to stop meddling and hindering progress, the other family members decided the answer was to sell the business.

In other instances, the family does not want to discuss or face obvious issues for fear of hurting a family member's feelings. Compensation is out of line, performance or contribution to the company is not what it should be, or someone is not cut out for the job. Many family businesses choose to overlook these areas of underperformance for the sake of maintaining family harmony.

Certainly, as any parent of young children can tell you, you need to choose your battles. Nothing is ever going to be perfect. But when the performance of the business is taking a dip because a family member is not adding value, should you allow it to continue?

The more common situation is not when the company is in trouble but when it is simply not reaching its potential. Everyone is getting paid, has plenty of vacation, and the business is making do with 2 percent net profit. Because everyone is "okay," it is more challenging to instigate the conversation with the family member whose contribution is holding the business hostage.

Answering this question is not as easy as it might seem. Ask the question another way: What if the business failed and the family succeeded?

If the family business collapsed as a direct result of the involvement or lack of involvement of a family member, then the only way back to harmony is simple forgiveness. You can't give the business another try; it is gone.

Alternatively, what would happen if the business succeeded and the family failed? Everyone made money, but no one shares Thanksgiving dinner together. While no one is happy about this, the opportunity would still exist every day to make things right.

> **Dirty Little Secret:** When it comes to family businesses, the whole can be greater than the sum of the parts.

What we know for a fact is that the most successful businesses are the ones that are run as businesses. However, we also know that those family businesses that have a high degree of trust and practice open and honest communication are the highest performing of all businesses. When it comes to family businesses, the whole can be greater than the sum of the parts.

Signs That It's Time to Sell the Family Business

Perhaps you have started to suspect you may need to sell your business rather than hand it down to your children. Here are a few indicators that you should consider selling the family business:

- **Your children don't want the business.** If you run a small retail shop that put your kids through college, the chances are they have their sights set on bigger goals when they graduate. The harder situation is when the company is big enough to warrant their joining the business, but they aren't interested. This can be painful when it happens. There is nothing wrong with laying out the facts regarding the opportunity that the family business presents to them. But forcing the company on your children will only result in either resentment or poor performance.

- **Your children are not capable.** I have unfortunately had many clients whose children, despite their parents' hopes and dreams, were not cut out to run the family business. My task was to bring the owner around to that idea. Sometimes there are circumstances where an outside leader can be brought in to run the business. But in that scenario, the question then becomes whether or not the kids can be good owners/managers.

- **Ownership has become too diluted.** Unless the company is always growing, it is hard to support a growing number of owners. This is true whether they work in the business or not, because the company winds up issuing dividends to those not in the business. Also, it could be a struggle to provide sufficient incomes to a large number of active owners. And there's also the increased difficulty in managing the business among multiple owners.

- **You receive an offer you can't refuse.** This was the situation with Anheuser-Busch, which was purchased by Belgian beverage giant InBev in 2008 for $52 billion. The offer was far beyond the realistic value of the business. And while the old guard tried to rationalize keeping the business, the current generation thought they would be foolish to turn down the offer. Don't try to convince yourself that you are keeping your company for your kids unless they understand the money involved, loudly declare their desire to run the business, and have a credible plan that makes financial sense.

- **Members of the next generation don't like working together.** Maybe all your kids are capable, but they can't seem to get along with each other. If they are not getting along now, it will only be worse once they are in business together. Rolling the business to them will impact your retirement plans, affect their lives, and possibly destroy any relationship they might have had.

- **There are major changes in your industry.** Market and technology changes can alter the business landscape such that it requires massive reinvestment to reposition the company. Sometimes it is just not worth that investment.

This is what happened to our family photography business, Olan Mills. People will always want a nice family portrait, but with everyone having a high-resolution camera on cell phones, the demand virtually collapsed.

You worked hard to build up the business. It would be wonderful if you could successfully pass it to the next generation. But sometimes the difficult but smart decision is to sell the family business.

> **Dirty Little Secret:** Sometimes the difficult but smart decision is to sell the family business.

Family-Owned Olan Mills Sold after Nearly Eighty Years

A few years ago, I received an unexpected phone call from my uncle, the chairman of Olan Mills. He was calling to tell me that our family business was being sold. If you are under thirty, you may not have heard of Olan Mills. But if you went to church or school, or had children or were a child in the sixties, seventies, or eighties there is a good chance you had your picture taken by an Olan Mills photographer.

My first reaction was sadness. The company had always been at the epicenter of our family and in many ways defined a part of each of us. But, understanding the photography industry and knowing that the buyer provided quality photos and valued their employees as Olan Mills did, I am comforted that it was a good sale.

My grandfather, Olan Mills, and his wife, Mary, started the company. Being the youngest of eleven children on a farm in hard times, he set out to make his own way. Family legend has it that he borrowed a camera from a friend and set up a sign on a street corner offering to take photographs. Five cents down and five cents when you came back for the picture.

A couple came along, plunked down their nickel, and my grandfather took their picture. When they returned the next day, he apologized that the pictures didn't turn out and said he would need to retake them. In reality, since he was broke, there had been no film in the camera—he needed that first five cents to buy the film. I call this American ingenuity.

Realizing he had struck upon something, he began going door-to-door offering to take pictures. The business grew so fast that he hired as many good salespeople as he could find. And at the end of the day, all the salespeople would come back to his house for dinner, many staying the night. It was truly a different era.

The true boost came when they began calling people by phone at home. It is a well-hidden fact that Olan Mills virtually invented telemarketing (sorry, everyone). However, it was a different model than what we know today. Olan Mills would use demographic data to locate a growing residential area and set up a studio. Then the company hired local employees to work in the studio to phone the lady of the house at appropriate times.

With this model in place, Olan Mills was well positioned to benefit from the baby boom. Studios could not be set up fast enough. The headquarters was in Chattanooga, Tennessee, with manufacturing facilities in Springfield, Ohio, and Dallas, Texas.

My grandparents had four children. Their two sons Olan and CG joined the company, and their two daughters (one of whom was my mother) did not. Olan Mills II, the oldest child, was in the business the longest. My uncle Olan began running a piece of the company after college. "One of the great aspects of being in a family business is that you have the opportunity to take on big responsibilities early in your career," my uncle reflected.

The company grew to more than a thousand studios across the country and expanded into the United Kingdom and Canada. In the late eighties, however, the company's fortunes began to turn. Telemarketing was getting a black eye because of rampant inappropriate usage, ultimately resulting in the Telephone Consumer Protection Act. This curtailed Olan Mills' ability to directly target new families. Then digital photography also began making great strides in quality and miniaturization. While an experienced photographer with a high-quality camera can never be replaced by amateur digital photography, millions of cell phone cameras in people's hands will affect demand.

So I am not sad about the sale. Yes, the company where I earned my first paycheck is no more. But it made a good living for my family and thousands of employees, and it provided cherished memories for millions of people for nearly eighty years.

Blood, Tears, and Whether to Sell

It's rumored that when InBev offered $52 billion in 2008 to buy Anheuser-Busch—the brewer of Budweiser—August Busch IV, the fifth-generation Busch to lead the family business, told his father that he did not want to sell the company but they would simply be crazy not to accept an offer that high.

I am sure most of us would accept that offer faster than we'd hit the road to the beach if our Friday meetings got canceled. But then most business owners don't have a business worth tens of billions or even tens of millions.

Nonetheless, many business owners suffer through deep consternation when faced with the prospect of selling their business. The simple remembrance of all the blood, sweat, and tears you, your parents, and maybe your grandparents spent building your business make it seem like heresy to throw it all away for a wad of cash.

And while some people can part with the business and never look back, many others sell their company for a pretty penny only to find that life after business is not what they thought it would be.

While the goal of Family Business USA is to continue the family business to the next generation, some family businesses should not or cannot survive. When I was in Cape Town, South Africa, a few years ago, I met a gentleman who was running a vineyard on the family farm. While it broke his heart, he knew that in the future there would not be a Sonnenberg running the farm that had been in the family for over a hundred years: He and his wife had no kids, and all his relatives had left the country.

If your children are happy and successful in careers outside the family business, should you disrupt that? Of course, the harder issue is when your sons or daughters would love to have the business, but you know in your heart that they simply don't have what it takes.

There is a unique situation where it is highly advisable to sell the business quickly. This occurs when the owner of the company is the heart, soul, and mind of the business and suddenly dies or becomes severely disabled. In this case, there is typically no one designated or prepared for leadership and no strong management team.

When the business moves to a wife or children who are not in the business and know little about it, they are overwhelmed. The longer they wait to sell, the more the business will decline and the lower the value they will receive when they face reality and sell it. Hopefully there was insurance.

At the same time, it would be foolhardy to sell your family business as a knee-jerk reaction to dealing with frustration such as:

- You are tired of the hassles of the business.
- Your kids are not cooperating with your plan.
- Your sibling sees the business differently.

Yes, these are painful issues, but maybe the business is not the root cause, or perhaps you would be trading one set of problems for another.

Selling a business is not a simple math equation. It is an irreversible life choice. "The best career, life, and business choices are made when there is harmony and balance between the rational mind and the emotional heart," says Rich Conners, the owner of Primarity Resources. "As such, it is critical to go through a process of capturing, defining, and prioritizing the most critical elements that are of the highest personal value to you and your family, in addition to running the numbers on the value of your business."

> **Dirty Little Secret:** Selling a business is not a simple math equation. It is an irreversible life choice.

Along these same lines, Princeton University recently performed a study that determined that additional income—up to about $75,000 a year—can increase an individual's happiness. Then the happiness plateaus.[1] So there *is* empirical evidence that money does not buy happiness. If you are considering selling your business, perform the due diligence on the financial side and get some good advice.

[T]here is empirical evidence that money does not buy happiness.

But the advice I would give you now is this: Dedicate the time and energy to understanding and getting comfortable with the idea of life after the family business. Selling your family business is a life-changing event. It affects a lot of people, and it is forever.

---

1 Belinda Luscombe, "Do We Need $75,000 a Year to Be Happy?" *Time*, September 6, 2010, http://content.time.com/time/magazine/article/0,9171,2019628,00.html.

The Next Generation Doesn't Want the Business— Now What?

Perhaps you are a member of the next generation and are not interested in taking on the company. How should you deal with this? Family business owners can become emotionally attached to their companies. When it comes time for Mom and Dad to start thinking about getting out, it can be difficult.

For many family business owners, the most desired option is to hand off the business to a family member, especially one who's been working in the business. On a financial note, it is also certainly much easier to handle an estate by passing the business to the next generation than being forced to sell.

So what does this have to do with breaking the news to your parents that you don't want their business? Everything. The best way to communicate a difference of desire with someone is to be able to understand their point of view and clearly articulate that to them. Convey to your parents that you've given the matter deep thought, and you're not taking the decision lightly.

You must have good reasons for not wanting to take over the company. But if you've been working in the business for many years, rotated through the departments, been successful, and are respected by the employees, you're pulling the rug out from under your parents if you suddenly decide it is not for you.

It's ideal to have open communication from the beginning: Let your parents know along the way that you're unsure about wanting to own the business one day. Tell your parents that you want to work in the business and would like to be paid and promoted according to the contribution you're making to the company, and that you're interested in potentially taking over one day. But tell them you also have an interest in opportunities outside the company. In other words, at this point, you're undecided.

Dirty Little Secret: It's ideal to have open communication from the beginning.

Sit down once a year to revisit the discussion so everyone is on the same page. Be open about your concerns, whatever they may be. Then be prepared: Your parents may have arguments refuting your concerns.

The part that will require a steel backbone is to be true to yourself by not letting your parents push you into running the business if that's not what you want. It will only result in unhappiness for you—and your parents.

Clearly articulate that you understand the difficult position it puts them in, and you don't want it to be painful and wish it weren't. Offer to assist with the transition. Ask them to try to understand why you're leaving and that you're not trying to hurt them. Last, give it time. This is an emotional situation—all the logic in the world is not going to placate hurt feelings overnight.

Perhaps your dream job has come along outside the family business. If so, don't leave your parents in a lurch. The right thing to do is ensure you have a good backfill before you depart. Hire someone, train them, and have them stabilized before you leave.

If you've been in the business for a while, understand the business, and are well respected, consider being on the board or establishing one. Plan formal meetings four times a year to debrief the status of the company and provide input. Your parents will appreciate your input and be happy that you're still connected to the business. They may have a small hope that you'll come back (and who knows, maybe you will).

If you're leaving at the time your parents are considering retirement, actively assist with alternatives: maybe finding a head buyer for the business and leading the deal through to conclusion. Find a way to stick around until things settle. This is one of those times when you lean to the family side: What can you do to help your parents effectively retire?

The final factor to discuss is your shares of the business. If you and your siblings outside the business all have the same number of shares, there may not be an issue. But if you have shares that were given in anticipation of you taking over the business, you may need to sell or give those shares back to the company. If you want to leave on good terms, arrange for no financial gain on your part and no financial impact to the company.

This is one of the best ways to say you are leaving: *I am your child, I love you, and I will help you with whatever I can. But this is my life, and I want to pursue my own dreams.*

CHAPTER 8

The Reins Change Hands

Graduation day, your first real job, your wedding day, the day your first child is born, and awards for achievements—these are the milestones of life for many people.

For a family business, the day the leadership passes from one generation to the next is the significant event. There are many ways that leadership can be handed over to the next generation. It can be planned or a surprise; it can be bumpy or smooth. You might envision the handover to the next generation being ushered in with a marching band and a fireworks display. In some cases this is true. But the best way is when you barely notice it at all.

More typical leadership transfer styles are outlined in the 1989 article in *Family Business Review* by Jeffrey Sonnenfeld and P. L. Spence. (See page 162 in the next section.) My favorite example is "the Monarch"; when the king dies, the next generation can assume control. Usually this is disastrous, with heirs squabbling and the eventual leader trying to adjust to sitting at the desk where the buck stops.

Sometimes an emergency prompts the move. A former client experienced a situation in which the current generation had a severe falling out, and the best resolution was to simply move the leadership to the next generation. While it occurred rather quickly, the next generation had been in the process of preparing for the transition already. Although it was earlier than planned, it was not a complete shock to the system.

The beautiful successions, however, are surprisingly smooth and as natural as you could imagine. One of my favorites was with a son who had managed each of the departments and had worked with banks, vendors, and customers. He had taken on significant business issues and opened up an entirely new route to market. He had read the books and attended the conferences.

The idea was certainly out there that at some point a transition would occur. But with his father still at the top of his game, there was no sense of urgency. It happened during a simple organizational restructuring meeting with the son and the dad. Some employees had left the company, and some people needed to be moved up while others needed to be moved over. In the cascading effect created by the reorganization, the question was raised, "What about Allen?"

Allen was one of those unique employees that they couldn't live with but they also couldn't live without. He was challenging to manage. "If we move him to the new position, who should he report to?" was the question.

"Well, he and I get along great," the son volunteered. "He could report to me."

That is when I interjected, "Well, then I suppose that would mean we would need to make you president."

There was a long silence before the son said, "Well, I guess so."

To which the dad, after a pregnant pause, responded, "Sounds good to me."

And it was done. The leadership had just changed hands.

People often ask me how you know when the best time is to change the leadership. The answer is simple: when everyone is ready. We'll discuss how to set yourself up for this change in leadership, with tips for making sure it is done right.

Ways to Approach Your Exit

As I've written before, much of the focus on family business transition is on whether the next generation can and will step up to the challenge. This is important to be sure; if you are stepping out of the business and there is no one assuming the leadership role, everything you've built may go to dust. Let's assume that the next generation is motivated and qualified to take over the business. In this case, the only thing standing in the way is *you*, the current business owner. The standard retort I hear from the current generation is, "Yes, I want to take some more time off, but I still want and need to be involved in the business. I don't want to just be cast out." In many cases, the immediate departure of the current leadership would be detrimental to the future success of the business.

There is one quite simple but effective strategy to transition yourself out of the business: Start taking every Friday off. Doing so will give you a three-day weekend and allow the next generation a little space to find their leadership footing. After some time of doing that, start taking Thursdays off also. Keep heading in this direction until you only come into the office late every Monday morning to have a cup of coffee.

> **Dirty Little Secret:** There is one quite simple but effective strategy to transition yourself out of the business: Start taking every Friday off.

However, also consider the following five approaches to exit strategies, from Jeffrey Sonnenfeld and P. L. Spence in their article "The Parting Patriarch of a Family Firm,"[1] as you think about your exit plan:

1. **The Monarch:** How does the king transition power to the next generation? He dies. This certainly is the most risky method of family business transition. Certainly, this is not a method that is thoughtfully and proactively selected as a business leadership transference strategy. Rather, it stems from the current leader's unwillingness to relinquish control, even though there will be negative consequences for such action. If the next generation is not capable of assuming leadership, elevate someone internally who is capable, bring someone in from the outside, or sell.

2. **The General:** At a predesignated date not of their choosing, generals are asked to retire. However, they may not be personally ready or still believe that they have value to add—or, worse, believe that no one can do it but them. This is common in family businesses. Mom or Dad will travel, play some golf, and either grow bored or elicit responses from their old guard that the next generation is not cutting it, thus setting

---

1 Jeffrey Sonnenfeld and Padraic L. Spence, "The Parting Patriarch of a Family Firm," *Family Business Review*, December 1989, vol. 2 no. 4, 355–375, doi:10.1111/j.1741-6248.1989.tb00004.x

the stage for them to come back to the rescue. And then they go away and come back, and go away and come back again, thus scuttling the opportunity for the next generation to get leadership footing.

3. **The Ambassador:** This exit style is commonly associated with highly functioning family businesses. Say Dad was progressively taking a day off a week until he was only coming by on Mondays for coffee. What would also happen is that when there were big contracts out for bid, a major issue at work, or simply opportunities or issues that were based on past relationships, Dad would arrive in a suit and tie ready to lend credibility and grease the path if necessary.

4. **The Governor:** This style is effective in larger organizations. It also works when the current generation truly does want to get out of the business and move on or to break company homeostasis, forcing the next generation to step up. Set a firm departure date in the future, and then begin working toward making everything happen by that date. While GE is not a family business, this was the famous exit strategy used by Jack Welch.

5. **The Inventor:** This style is where the leader gives up lead of the business but still contributes in the particular area he can offer expertise.

More than 65 percent of family businesses fail to make it to the next generation. This leads us to believe that the fault and blame for the failure is completely on the next generation. *It's not!* The current generation has at least 50 percent responsibility because they either hang on so long that the next generation never gets quality time in the driver's seat or so long that they start making bad decisions that damage the company.

> **Dirty Little Secret:** More than 65 percent of family businesses fail to make it to the next generation.

Now Is the Time to Plan Your Exit Strategy

Say there are two brothers and the wife of one of the brothers all running the family business together, and all are ready to get out. Once the next generation gets there, how will the three members of the current generation know when and how to leave the business?

Clearly, the first hurdle is financial. Does the business generate enough profit or have enough assets so that it can fund retirement? This depends on how much wealth you think you need for the rest of your life. If the business is generating no profit, has no assets that can be sold or downsized, and you're taking $60,000 in salary, you will be hard pressed to sell the business to anyone at a price you can retire on.

Once you've passed that hurdle, ask yourself and the other owners, "Do we want to see the business continue into the next generation?" This is different from "Am I okay with the next generation owning the business?" There needs to be a true desire on behalf of the current generation to see the business passed to the next generation.

We are assuming, of course, that the next generation is ready, willing, and able to take over the business. This question needs to be asked when there is a financial need to extract some value out of the company in order to fund retirement.

Let's say your personal financial dreams are quite different from your spouse's or brother's. What should you do? This is where good communication and a good financial planner are essential. With a husband and wife team, it's vital to go together to a fee-only certified financial planner. These are professionals who have experience doing the math on your current personal wealth, business assets, and the income and spending wants and needs through life, so you can be confident that you will have enough money after you exit the business. Going together is important so that you work from the same data set to discuss what type of retirement you desire.

The fly in the ointment can be the third partner. His financial objectives can be different from yours. This is where negotiation, compromise, and respectful communication are essential.

There are nonfinancial objectives as well. The biggest one is how you will be affected by no longer being the person in charge of the company. There is an enormous amount of self-esteem and activity that comes with running a company—even more so when it's a company you've built. Many business owners sell, only to find that financial independence doesn't satisfy the psychological need to be a part of something. Rich Conners, founder of Primarity Resources, is an expert in helping business owners work through selling their business. According to Conners, "There are four aspects that must be considered when considering selling your business: your life goals, your future living, the company legacy, and exit readiness."

Along these same lines, you want to be sure that all stakeholders in the business are pleased with the transition or sale. How will the transition of the business affect your employees, especially the long-term ones? How will it impact the community? How will it impact your broader family?

When there is more than one owner, exiting can be tricky. If both want to leave, who should leave first? Usually, this is solved by circumstances: One of the owners wants or needs to leave immediately and can. From a desired sequence perspective, all but the true leader should exit first. This allows the rest of the organization to stabilize before the exit of the leader.

> **Dirty Little Secret:** When there is more than one owner, exiting can be tricky.

Another tricky aspect of transition often encountered in family businesses is when there are two or more siblings in the business and the leader is ready to get out. In this situation, it's common for one of the siblings to want to take a shot at running the company. However, "getting my shot at it" is insufficient grounds for putting someone in the top position. It is tempting to allow your cousin or sibling to have an opportunity to drive the car, so to speak. You are backing out and this is that person's chance to be at the head of the firm, make some changes, and garner some of the prestige that comes along with a fancy title. This is where many family businesses can trip up and make a decision based on family emotion, instead of business logic. If it makes business sense, then great, go for it. But if not, you will be better off installing and grooming the next generation (and designating your sibling as the primary mentor for now).

A better method is to allow the next generation, if they are ready, to assume control while the other siblings continue on. This minimizes the number of transitions and the disruption each causes and gives great support to the next-generation leadership, enabling long-term success. (With this said, there have been many family businesses in which the siblings or spouses are both at such a high skill and leadership level that one could leave and the other could easily take over.)

One situation that often causes problems for family businesses is when multiple siblings each have children. It is a given that parents will want their children to do well and succeed. And while any parent would assist his child in finding a job by referring her to a friend or acquaintance who is hiring, when siblings in a family business are watching out for their best interests and those of their own children, there will likely be conflicts of interest. If all the siblings are trying to give their kids the plum assignments, increase their pay, push for their promotions, and go light on their performance reviews, a train wreck is waiting to happen when it comes time to figure out which current-generation members can lead the company.

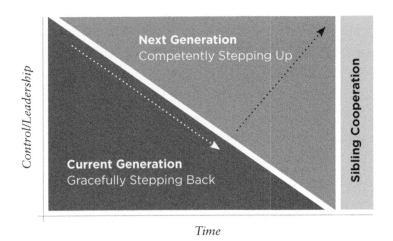

Figure 8.1 Hidden Landmine—Sibling Cooperation

Handing the Company to the Next Generation

The first question to ask yourself: *Am I selling or giving my business to the next generation?* More likely than not, you are selling, but at a favorable discount. There are two types of valuations you can have performed on your business: one to pass it to the next generation (lower) and the other to pass it to a strategic buyer (higher).

If you are handing off a family business to more than one heir, it can become awkward. If you don't handle the transaction correctly, you could unintentionally set up the next generation to fail. It is best practice for the leader of the family business to have a majority ownership over the others; shared leadership is slow and difficult to manage, especially if there is a clear leader—or those who clearly are not leaders. Monetarily it can almost be meaningless, but from a control perspective it can mean the success or failure of the family business. Many parents are unwilling to structure the ownership this way because they would be uncomfortable explaining the structure to the potential minority shareholders. However, if the clear leader does not have slightly greater control, the business could be stifled, resulting in frustration among all owners.

When working through succession—and even during everyday operations—it is a mistake to neglect or not pay full attention to family members who are outside the family business. When thinking of succession and estate planning, you must fully consider the ramifications on all family members regardless of whether they work in the family business. The baseline is that if the business were sold, and there were only cash in the bank, the estate would be divided equally among your heirs. It does not necessarily have to be exactly this way when there is a big asset like a business, but failure to fully address the financial and psychological needs of family members who work elsewhere can set up the family business to hit a brick wall down the road. Sometimes family members who are owners but who work elsewhere may force advice on those who are running the family business or demand unreasonable returns.

> **Dirty Little Secret:** When thinking of succession and estate planning, you must fully consider the ramifications on all family members regardless of whether they work in the family business.

There are instances in which the heirs are sufficiently cooperative, in addition to being willing and able, so you can give them equal ownership, or where all the wealth is wrapped up in the business and this is the only way to provide equal wealth. In any case, it is imperative that a good buy-sell agreement is established.

A good buy-sell agreement will enable dissatisfied business partners to get out of the company and receive a fair price for their shares. It will also ensure that ownership is not sold on the open market, and it protects the other owners from potentially being in business with another owner's wife or heirs if that owner were to die. In the case of a death, life insurance can provide a good liquidity cushion.

The greatest benefit a buy-sell agreement provides is the peace of mind that if things were to go awry, you could safely get out of the business. Interestingly, having this knowledge keeps many sibling partners working together successfully over the long term.

The next consideration: *Who am I passing the business to, and who am I not passing it to?* The best answer here is to always try to put it in the hands of people who already work in the business. In order to foster greater success in the next generation of leadership, it is best to ensure they have control over the business.

One of my clients had a general manager who held only a minority of the shares, and none of the client's other family shareholders worked in the business. Under these circumstances, if the company wasn't performing to the level desired by those outside shareholders, they might start sticking their noses in the business in an effort to improve it, even though they knew nothing about it. And if you are a

C corporation, it can be more awkward, because dividends would be the only way to pay the other shareholders. Thus, the owners would also be forced to take dividends, but dividends are double taxed and the owner's salary may be more than sufficient.

In order to foster greater success in the next generation of leadership, it is best to ensure they have control over the business.

If you have adequate other wealth, it's best to simply equalize gifts of stock to family members working in the business with cash or other assets to those who are working outside the business. If you don't have the wealth, then a good life insurance policy can create enough liquidity at your death to enable those in the business to inherit the business and those who are outside to receive the cash. Without some liquidity, the financial pressure on those in the business may be so severe that they are forced into a panic sale.

If you are selling the company to family members working in the business, you don't have to completely equalize with their siblings unless you're selling the company at a lower value than you would on the open market. What is critically important is to ensure that all family members are aware of what's going on so no one is surprised later. Having a good family meeting can alleviate all of this.

Finding the Funding

So now you are lined up from a leadership and ownership perspective. Your next question is *Where is the money going to come from?* There are a variety of options:

- **Leveraged recapitalization:** The company can take debt from a lender, using company assets as collateral, and buy out a portion of the owner's shares. With a private equity firm, their interest will be in building up the value to have it resold. However, the next-generation heirs can also buy them out.
- **Joint venture:** Bring in an operating partner. If the new partner brings the skills, vision, and money, this can be a good option.
- **Noncontrol investment:** Sell a minority ownership stake in the company. If your business has a good track record of making a lot of cash, there are investors out there for whom this would be a good investment. But they will want a tight contract, and so should you.
- **Sale over time:** Having the next generation buy out over time is probably the most common option. This, of course, necessitates that they continue to run the company well so there is cash available to buy out the owner. Many times, the next generation can be forced to take out a loan to make this happen.

With any financial option, it is critical to clean up the books as much as possible. Have a strong financial person, have the books audited, and get all nonworking children off the payroll.

Unique Estate Planning Tool for Those Who Are "ABIL"[1]

Many times family business owners spend a lifetime building something special and of value only to have to fire sale all or part of it to pay taxes, which could leave less than 15 percent of your current wealth after taxes. At the same time, some owners buy life insurance using their own liquid assets to pay for life premiums, often triggering gift taxes and always incurring a significant opportunity cost. And many times the return on investment is only positive if the insured dies early—not an attractive option.

However, there is a unique financing tool available to some family business owners called ABIL, or asset-backed insurance lending. These transactions allow business owners or those with significant wealth to address their tax liability without having to liquidate the very assets they have spent a lifetime building. It enables you to control what is done with your assets when you die, without having the government decide for you. ABIL is about doing the planning and minimizing the cost while keeping control of most, if not all, of your assets.

1 Source: Grace Barnard, President of NIW Companies, www.niwcorp.com.

Show Them You Can Lead

As part of the transition, the next generation must be allowed to establish themselves within the business while the current generation is still involved. Are you looking to take over a family business soon?

One of the crucial elements to your success as the next generation managing the business is your ability to win over all constituencies: customers, suppliers, employees, and partners. You know the product and services. You've mastered the core functions. You've successfully and independently led significant projects and initiatives to completion. You've spent time being mentored by someone further down the road. You've had some advanced training and education in the industry. And, optimally, you've spent time working outside the family business. However, none of this connects you to the groups of people with whom you must have strong relationships in order to be successful.

A client of mine, a second-generation family business in construction, had developed a reputation for being the best. The two children in the business had the skills, knowledge, and motivation to be leaders in the company. But the real success of the business, the "secret sauce" if you will, was the strong relationships the current- and previous-generation leaders had developed with their partners and suppliers. In many ways, the success of the business depended on these relationships—the business network. In order for the next generation to be successful, they needed to begin gaining the network's trust to garner the benefits of good relationships.

The best approach to developing any relationship is to feel each other out. Carve out a bite-sized portion of responsibility for a project or a less critical function, and have Mom or Dad inform the customer or supplier that you will be handling this area. This enables the customer or supplier to gauge your performance quality without assuming all the risk. It's important to avoid communicating this change in the relationship yourself—it would convey that the customer's or supplier's relationship with the current ownership is not important enough to warrant a formal handoff. As the next generation, you would also run the risk of appearing arrogant and overconfident by announcing your own takeover.

The customer or supplier doesn't care how much you know until they know how much you care. You may be good at what you do, but the road is littered with people who were good yet couldn't connect with people. Being good at what you do is not enough to develop a strong relationship with customers and suppliers. It's more important to prove, establish, and develop a reputation for how you work—that you're reliable, trustworthy, dependable, communicative, and caring. The critical thing to remember is that you only get one chance at a first impression. If you can win over your customers and suppliers by overdelivering on small projects, they will be comfortable when you move to bigger responsibilities, and they will cut you slack if something happens to go wrong, because you've already built some trust.

> **Dirty Little Secret:** The customer or supplier doesn't care how much you know until they know how much you care.

While there needs to be a transition period in which your parents can introduce you as taking over some responsibilities, you certainly don't want to seem like Dad's sidekick. Prove that you have the capacity to stand on your own two feet and think for yourself. Set up one-on-one meetings with customers and suppliers to discuss topics relevant to them.

The seriousness of the work is not as important as demonstrating that you operate well independently and that you're not simply an extension of your parents.

Along similar lines, plan to attend some industry conferences solo. Look for opportunities to write published articles on industry topics and speak to or teach groups. Getting involved in industry-related initiatives demonstrates you're not a one-trick pony. It also gains you exposure.

Perhaps the most important aspect of helping your customers and suppliers see you as the future leader is to reach out to them directly. For a supplier, it can be as simple as taking the initiative to call and invite him to lunch or coffee to discuss ways to work more closely. For customers, staff the front door and greet them as they walk in. Introduce yourself and ask if you can help. It's a tried-and-true method of establishing a reputation as someone who cares. You could ask customers how you can be a better provider for them. Sure, there are myriad projects to be worked on, personnel issues to address, and crises to avert, but carving out a few days to meet customers will be worth the results. You can't meet and help everyone, but it has a meaningful impact on the people you touch, and they'll spread the word.

Finally, as you set out to make your own mark as the future leader of the company, remember one thing: While your parents may have a particular style that endeared them to their customers and suppliers, no one expects or wants you to be their clone. Yes, everyone wants reliability and quality products and service, but they also want trust and sincerity. Be yourself, have your own style, and double down on your own strengths. This is the best way to advertise to your customers and suppliers that there's a new leader on the way.

When the Baton Is Passed, Are You Ready to Run?

As the up-and-coming next-generation leader of the family business, there are many things that need to be done in order to smoothly transition the business. Some are not so obvious.

First, let's discuss what we mean by "transfer." From a business perspective, we tend to keep our eyes on the business and its current owner. This makes a lot of sense because, prior to the handoff, the business is and has been in fine, capable hands. So let's take a quick look at the receiver, or the next-generation owner.

Like in a relay race, the runners with the baton do not want to let go until they are sure the receivers have a good grip on it. This is exactly what the current generation thinks, too. However, the handoff, in this sense, occurs over years. You need to prove that you are capable of running the business before the owner lets go.

There are a few questions that need to be answered to determine if you are ready:

- **Do you have a sense of independence?** There is a saying that it is lonely at the top. Well, it is. There is no one to talk to about decisions you make. Certainly, there is plenty of input, but ultimately you must make the final decision. Can you say no in the face of strong opposition? Do you know what your values are? Have you said no to your dad, mom, or whoever is running the business? All of this is required to be a leader.

- **Are you fairly good at what you do?** If you are in a financial business and are not good with numbers, maybe the family business is not for you. But if there are aspects of it that appeal to you but others in which you are weak, spend time working to understand those aspects.

- **Are you a good communicator?** Can you speak and write fairly clearly? Are you confident when communicating in person? Can you tell people things they don't want to hear? At the same time, do you understand the importance of communication, and can you ensure that it happens on a regular basis?

- **Are you thinking ahead?** Where should the business be three, five, or ten years from now? How should we get there? What needs to change? In business, the ground underneath your feet is always changing. Can you keep up and even get ahead?

- **Are you evolving?** Are you constantly chasing down ways to improve yourself and be a better manager and leader? Are you a good listener? Do you seek out advice? Have you initiated a major project and seen it all the way through to completion, rising above setbacks?

The list can go on, but the point here is that the current generation is always evaluating you and will be looking at these types of characteristics and actions to gauge how prepared you are to take over leadership.

The next area involves lining up other external parties. Do your siblings and other key employees support the transition of the business over to you? You need to find out where they stand and what concerns they may have. In any business, there will be some highly qualified managers who have a good relationship with the current leader. You may have siblings who either work at the business or receive income from the business. They will want to know their situation will be okay if you move into the leadership role. If they need to be moved out in order for the next generation to be successful, you will need to work out all of that.

The biggest issue is what to do about Mom or Dad. From your perspective, it may seem as simple as saying, "Let me have your office." However, you need to truly appreciate the difficulty of stepping down. As such, it is important to define, over time, what your parents will be doing with themselves once they are not fully engaged in the company. This brings up the following three questions: What role do they have in the business now? What leadership roles will they have in the company after the "baton" is passed? What do they plan to do outside of work? While these questions can seem easy, they are not. Remember the issues we discussed with the various CEO exit styles.

The final steps in the transition revolve around retirement planning and ownership transfer. Needless to say, it's important that your parents have sufficient means to care for themselves. This can be handled through keeping Dad on to pull down a salary or buying him out. In the case of many family businesses in which real estate is involved, rent can be paid for the facilities.

However, the most important aspect of transference is to get the topic on the table as soon as it makes sense. Many family business owners struggle to leave the business because they are so emotionally wrapped up in it. They have trouble seeing their children try to run the business, and they have trouble letting go enough to allow the next generation to make the needed changes to the business.

As for ownership transfer, the question is, *Is there sufficient wealth or life insurance that would allow those who work in the business to inherit the business, while the other siblings receive cash?* If not, then you need to plan for your inactive siblings to have some ownership in the business. The best way to prepare for this is to have a meeting with your siblings, without your parents, to discuss everyone's perspective. Try to come to a unified agreement on how you would manage the relationship in the future and present it to your parents.

The greater sense you can convey to your parents that everything is handled on a personal, emotional, business, and family level, the easier the transition will be for everyone involved.

Ownership Transfer: Financial Aspects

When the time comes to transfer ownership, the standard method is simply to value the business and have the next generation buy the company, but this is easier said than done. Many times, the value of the business is beyond what the next generation can afford to pay, even over an extended period of time. A good question to ask is, *How much money do I actually need from the sale of the company?* There is a spectrum of answers, from "I need all the money. This is how I'm funding my retirement, and if the next generation doesn't get funding, then we need to talk about selling" to "I don't need the money, and I'm going to give away as much as I can without incurring a hefty tax burden." Most companies fall somewhere in between.

Many times, the value of the business is beyond what the next generation can afford to pay, even over an extended period of time.

In one client's experience, the current generation bought the business from the founding generation for less than what the business was worth. The founder wanted to see the business get to the next generation, and while he needed some retirement money from the business, he didn't need the amount the business was actually worth. Ultimately, the number was a valuation that was as low as possible without alerting the IRS that there was a gift that would require taxation.

It is important to understand the difference between capital gains taxes, which are taxes on selling assets, and income taxes, which are taxes on money made from using those assets. Because the capital gains tax rate is much lower than the income tax rate, if you were planning on sticking around the company and continuing to pull in an income after the sale, don't. You and the business would be better off bumping up the price of the stock and lowering the amount of income you'd receive in the future—which, of course, would be none.

> **Dirty Little Secret:** It is important to understand the difference between capital gains taxes and income taxes.

In certain industries, there is the added issue of the land the business sits on. Many times the land is worth more than the business itself or, at least, is quite valuable. Depending on the type of business, however, moving locations can be damaging to the company. This is a common issue in many family businesses: having a valuable asset that, if sold, could fund a nice retirement but would rip the heart out of the business. A possibility here is to simply buy the business and land over time.

It is important to consider what you're leaving to your children who are not in the business. If the next generation is buying the business and all the assets at a true market value, then there is nothing to discuss. But, to the degree that you manipulate the value down or gift part of it, you need to consider how you will balance this with your other children. This is when a good life insurance policy can be the answer, creating liquidity for other family members.

In many family businesses, the next generation consists of more than just one child. How will you handle two children of equal skill levels and contributions to the business? Certainly, one answer is 50/50. However, sometimes this can suboptimize the operations of the business if two people have to agree on every strategic decision. Another alternative is to give a slight majority to one, but then put a good buy-sell in place to ensure the minority can get out at a fair price if desired. You can even make a cash gift to the one who receives the minority to compensate. The point here is not that you love one child more than another, but that usually the business will operate better with a single decision maker, which will make everyone better off.

There is a family business I know of where the founders gave 100 percent ownership to one son, even though two other sons were working in the business. The business is doing great, and the three brothers all get along wonderfully. Clearly, the owner son is such a high performer that his two brothers realize that if they line up behind him, they will also do well—and they have.

So where does the money come from to buy the business? Typically there is a buyout over time, with perhaps a chunk up front. Sometimes the business has to shrink a bit in order to fund the buyout. However, there are other options: the bank or private equity. If your company has had little debt and consistent income over the years and can demonstrate that the next generation has already been running the business, a bank may lend you the money. Another option: If there is an interesting growth plan, you may try securing private equity. This type of arrangement will certainly have a higher payback threshold, but if the growth prospects are good, financially it can work out. There are private equity firms out there that specialize in lending to family businesses with the end goal of getting the business back into the hands of the family.

Another option is an employee share ownership plan (ESOP). Essentially this is a qualified retirement plan through which employees receive shares of the corporation's stock. The benefit of an ESOP is that it allows the shareholder to sell shares to the ESOP entity and avoid taxes, and the company can borrow money through the ESOP and then repay the loan through fully tax-deductible contributions. These tax savings can be significant. However, ESOPs are expensive to set up, so the value of the company has to be large enough to make it worthwhile. At the same time, the company needs to be profitable in order to gain from the tax savings. Finally, the seller's time horizon has to be long enough to benefit.

Financial Considerations for the Next-Generation Owner

For the next-generation owners, there are also financial considerations. What steps do you need to take to assure the transition of the business from the first generation to your ownership is as smooth as possible? There are a number of important things to consider.

First, you should get a professional valuation from a certified expert to help you understand how much the business is worth. This doesn't necessarily mean it is the price you'll pay for the company, but it does provide an external and impartial value of the business. And this isn't the only reason a professional valuation is important.

The IRS will want its piece. Let's say the business is worth $10 million, but Mom and Dad charge you only $7 million. The IRS views the $3 million difference as a gift with possible taxes due. Then, let's say your parents have died, and the IRS does a review and discovers the discrepancy. Guess who pays the taxes? You. Guess who won't have the liquidity at the moment? You. Guess who is forced into a fire sale of the business? You guessed it: you!

The good news is there is a recognized range of valuations. For example, the value of a business to a strategic buyer would bring the highest value. A strategic buyer is a business that needs another business to complete its portfolio, enter a new market, or block a competitor from getting into the market. Think of Microsoft buying Skype for $8.5 billion, even though Skype lost $7 million the previous year and had about the same amount in debt. Microsoft didn't want Google or Facebook to get their hands on Skype.

Through a more simplified financial analysis, without strategic buyers waiting in the wings, how much is the business worth? Get a valuation from a certified professional and inform them that you need the valuation for the purpose of transferring the business to the next generation, you. That way, if the IRS has a question, the onus is on the valuation professional to justify the price.

As mentioned, if the plan is to be co-owners with your siblings or anyone else, it is wise to establish a buy-sell agreement with a valuation process defined. This way, if someone wants to leave the company, the separation process will already be understood.

Another critical step in understanding the financial ramifications of buying the company from the first generation is developing solid financial skills yourself, as the new next-generation owner. The best way to gain these skills is by spending a stint as the chief accountant, with the responsibility of generating the monthly financial statements. If this isn't possible, sit down once a month to review financial statements in detail with your CFO and attend some financial statement analysis courses. You should also get advice from qualified financial professionals, but considering the importance of the topic, having your own understanding is critical.

As a part of this process, you will need to reconcile how all the siblings will be treated. For example, if they are in the business, how should ownership be divided? Remember, equal is not always better. Also be sure there is a good buy-sell agreement defining the terms under which any owner can sell shares of the company. It can save your business and your relationships. If the siblings are not in the business, then ownership usually should be avoided if there is sufficient liquidity to balance out any gifts. As mentioned, one way to assist with this is for the current generation to have adequate life insurance.

The next step in preparing to take over the business is to be involved in the estate planning of your parents. In many regards, this is the last step in the development process. There are two critical elements for this to go smoothly: having the relationship, trust, and healthy communication to be involved and having the knowledge to assist. When it comes to the relationship, it is vital to understand that you may not see eye to eye with your parents on their needs and desires after they retire or when they die. It can be a delicate situation.

Assuming you have the relationship to be involved in the estate planning process, get yourself up to speed with the various aspects of estate planning, including insurance, investing, tax ramifications, and legalities.

There may be other family members involved in this process as well, including siblings in and outside the business. The estate plan will need to treat each sibling in a fair and equitable manner. Business ownership is a key area to consider. If family members are not working in the business, it doesn't mean they should get shares of the business because they are family. This is only considered, usually, if there is no other liquidity available, or the liquidity available is too important for the growth of the business.

Now, after all this, you'll likely still need to buy the business from your parents. If they are financially secure, it's in their best interest to get the purchase price as low as legally possible. Then, they can gift you up to the maximum tax-free amount and pay gift tax after that level. However, if your parents aren't financially independent, you'll need to purchase some or all of the business.

I mentioned some funding possibilities earlier, but another exotic funding mechanism is a *captive*, which involves setting up your own insurance company to fund the insurance needs of your company. You can own or partially own the insurance company. Over a period of time, the insurance company can shut down, leaving the owners with the proceeds and extraordinary tax savings. Again, this is highly sophisticated and shouldn't be entered into lightly.

Finally, if you don't have a board of advisors, put one in place. Get three to five people who are fully independent of the company and its stakeholders but who have knowledge that can be helpful to the business. Having at least one member with strong financial experience would be wise. This will provide you with a good sounding board as you go through the transition process, from business, family, and financial perspectives.

CHAPTER 9

Setting Up New Owners for Success

The day has come when it is time to change seats. Perhaps the transfer of ownership is a smooth transition in which your mom and dad take on different roles and step away from the day-to-day activities of running the family business. Or maybe it happened suddenly, even under sad or unfortunate circumstances. Whether the move happened gradually or suddenly, there are steps that need to be taken right now in order for your company to move forward and prosper. In this chapter we'll look at strategies next-generation owners can use to successfully take on the family business.

Get In the Know

Get good financial information and understand it. You are in business to make a dollar, and the measuring stick to determine profitability is your financial statement. If you do not have a good accountant and good accounting practices, fix it now. Building a business on bad financials is like building a house on sand: It doesn't matter how good the house is. It will always have problems. At the same time, make sure you can read the financials well enough to make informed decisions. They are the control panel of your company. If you don't understand them, take a managerial accounting course.

In terms of on-the-job training, the first step is to do a good rotation through the company departments. This is like studying a book that you need to absorb. Instead of just flipping through, read a good portion of each chapter. This will give you the opportunity to see how the business works as a system.

But it's not only about the business process; it's also about the people: the colleagues you work with, the vendors who supply you with the products you sell, and most important, the customers who buy your products. Get to know and understand each of these groups, finding out what's important to them.

The next step is to get deeply into the industry. From a learning perspective, it is critical to attend trade shows and conferences. There are three major learning opportunities at industry events. First, meeting with vendors can help you understand all the products and services available and enable you to compare the options. Next, keynote talks and seminars are designed to train and educate you about the various facets of business. Finally, other company operators are on hand to answer questions or discuss any challenges you may have in your business. Work toward continuous development. You must continually educate yourself. It's easy, after many years of being in the business, to think you've seen it all and know everything, but ongoing education is essential.

Reading is one simple step you can take. Magazines are good because they give you quick information. Read industry-specific titles as well as general business magazines such as

Bloomberg Business Week. In addition, pick up business books about business strategy, marketing, other industries, and other related topics. They could spur broader and more strategic thought on actions that you should take at your company.

Dirty Little Secret: Work toward continuous development.

Course work is another avenue you could use to build your knowledge. If you want to be successful running a company these days, it is best to have some business education. If you have an undergraduate degree in business, that should suffice, but if you don't, consider an MBA program. If this isn't possible, take these five courses: accounting, finance, operations management, marketing, and economics. Don't neglect small courses on topics where you lack confidence or those of special interest to your business.

Don't neglect small courses on topics where you lack confidence or those of special interest to your business.

Networking groups are also helpful resources that can produce valuable information from your peers. If you are under the age of forty-five, seek out the Young Presidents' Organization (YPO) group in your area. Otherwise, think about joining a Vistage executive coaching group. Both cost money, but they enable you to share your leadership challenges with other leaders. Then there are standard networking groups like Rotary and Chamber of Commerce. Toastmasters is also an excellent resource to improve speaking skills.

Seek outside advice. Networking groups will take you a long way, but they can only go so deep into your particular situation. Many business leaders, especially newer ones, find benefits in enlisting the help of business coaches, consultants, and mentors. Jack Welch, the revered former leader of General Electric Company, had a personal business coach so that someone sharp, who didn't work for him, would talk to him straight.

Own Your New Role

Realize that *you are the leader now.* This means a few things. Congratulations are in order for you, but now is not the time to rest on your laurels. On the contrary, this is the hard part. Up to this point, you were simply a passenger in the car—now your hands are on the wheel. You are in charge, and the buck stops with you. Remember, it is lonely at the top. Smart and experienced people will give you advice, but ultimately it is up to you to make the tough decisions. Here is a list of some tried-and-true advice:

- **Accept that mistakes are okay.** Many leaders get hung up trying to either be perfect or appear perfect. This can create an environment in which others think that they, too, must be perfect, which means they could take steps to cover up their mistakes. The goal of a business is to make money, and the business landscape is always changing. You need to always be improving, which requires some mistakes.

- **Establish your own contacts and relationships.** To get your company to where it is now, your parents or the former owners had a network of folks they would rely on: CPAs, lawyers, and insurance brokers, as well as others in the industry and some outside the industry. You don't have to jettison these relationships. In fact, you should keep them all, but you need to determine for yourself who you are going to rely on for information and advice.
- **Hire the best.** One of the best famous pieces of business advice is to hire people who are smarter than you. Similar to being willing to make a mistake, this requires putting aside your ego.
- **Plan your time wisely.** Remember, your time is valuable, so manage it effectively. Take the time to train people so that you can delegate. Try to structure your day so you can focus on certain activities in an allotted time frame: email for an hour, return phone calls for an hour, etc. Multitasking allows you to touch many things shallowly. Focus enables depth, which yields higher quality work and is ultimately more efficient.
- **Make your company about the people.** Remember that business is about people. Create a sense of team. Motivate and encourage people, and allow them a chance to voice and deploy their ideas. The more people feel a sense of ownership, the more they will go the extra mile. Remember your emotional intelligence—gauge the feelings of others, be aware of your own, and be sure to listen.

It is your company now to shape as you see best. Over time, shake off the way it has been done in the past, and make the business successful in the future. You are in the driver's seat—now drive the car.

Leadership Is Key

Now I'm going to shift gears. My intention is not to teach you how to run a business but how to become a good owner. The difference is that the owner is singularly responsible for the company and everything about it.

There are myriad theories, books, and courses on leadership development, but I'm going to condense leadership and ownership mentality to these nine important elements:

1. **Communicate.** Listen first, understand, then ensure the right frequency and depth of communication with everyone you depend on and who depends on you. Consider Toastmasters International, a nonprofit organization designed to assist in developing public speaking and leadership skills.
2. **Admit mistakes, and accept criticism.** It is imperative that people are willing to tell you what you don't want to hear and that you listen to them. Arrogance does nothing for you or your business.
3. **Plan ahead, prioritize, and focus on the important, not the urgent.** Business comes at you fast. Look down the road to see what's coming, and have a framework for what to work on now and what to leave for later.

4. **Develop people skills.** Business is people, and you need to be able to motivate them to help you.

5. **Work on 360-degree continual growth: mind, body, spirit, and business.** You should always be reading a nonfiction book. Also, make it a point to read a general interest magazine, such as *Time*, and a business magazine, such as *BusinessWeek* or the *Wall Street Journal*, regularly.

6. **Cast a broad net and seek leadership opportunities.** Always network, and not just in your industry. Try your local chamber of commerce, church, Lions Clubs, Rotary Clubs, and other nonprofit organizations.

7. **Carve out a piece of the business and manage the entire entity from a profit and loss (P&L) responsibility.** It doesn't matter where the responsibility is as much as having the responsibility.

8. **Be proactive but patient.** There's a difference between taking action and being overly pushy or demanding. In the same breath, there's a difference between not paying attention and waiting for something to develop. It's a delicate balance.

9. **Have an open and ongoing dialogue with the current (or past) owners.** They are in a different stage of life and have different priorities than you. As such, it is important to have honest communication about their goals and your goals, and how each of you sees a transition evolving.

Becoming a successful owner is a process that never ends. By learning through the right training, education, and experience, you will get there.

It's Time to Open the Door to the Next Generation's Ideas

When most family-owned companies are started, no one is thinking about how the business will continue into the next generation. The focus is on getting the business off the ground and stabilized to generate a reliable return. With one estimate showing that 50 percent of new businesses will fail in five years, and more than 70 percent in ten years,[1] the odds are intimidating. The risk for founders is high.

However, through the years, the creative, persistent, and sometimes risky problem solving that is the secret to success is often abandoned as the business grows. The more success that is gained, the less risk the owner is willing to take on. This can lead to stagnation, rigidity, and even decline, unless steps are taken and the owner remains flexible.

For a company to be successful into the next generation, new ideas are essential.

For a company to be successful into the next generation, new ideas are essential. The world around us is always changing, and it takes a level of creativity to keep up. For example, one family-owned retailer I know swears that establishing a dog food business inside their garden

---

1 Small Business Association, "What Is the Survival Rate for New Firms," Frequently Asked Questions, https://www.sba.gov/sites/default/files/sbfaq.pdf.

supply store has been instrumental in maintaining long-term relevance. And we all know of retailers that have incorporated food services in order to bring in more customers. While these two ideas may not be right for your store, you need to create an environment in which other new ideas are welcome.

The obstacle to creating this kind of open-mindedness lies both with the owner and the next generation.

The difficulty with the owner is that, as time goes on, there is a psychological and rational reason to begin consolidating and securing for the future. Ever increasingly, growth stocks are moved into bonds or dividend-bearing equities. Owners are inherently reluctant to change the business and are resistant to radical change. But ideas about change lead to actual change only when they are not stomped out.

Let's look at family business owners. They are in charge. As the leaders, they can best see how a change here could impact something over there. They have years of experience and have seen what does and doesn't work. They built the business—it's their baby, and they're depending on the income.

For the next generation, bringing an idea to the table can be quite intimidating. It probably will not be perfect, and all the cons will be pointed out. Feelings can easily get hurt, and discouragement can set in.

At one company I worked with, I noticed that one of the senior managers seemed disinterested in discussions about the future. When I asked why, the response was, "I tried to get involved when I first started, but I got my hand slapped so many times, I decided to just focus on my work.

And since I'm retiring in the next ten years, whatever happens can't really affect me."

If the owner is truly interested in the company moving forward, it is necessary to begin handing over some control and allow the next generation to get the creative juices flowing and shape it in their own way. But the problem with the next generation is that years of doing things the owner's way may inhibit ingenuity.

To foster an atmosphere of openness and originality, it is important for the owner to understand where the next generation is coming from, including these considerations:

- The next-generation owners are going to have their own style, which will be different from yours. But that doesn't make it bad. In fact, research shows it's good. The future is different from the past, and the style of the past may not be effective in the future.
- The next generation needs to make the business their own. The difference between the passenger seat and the driver's seat has a profound psychological impact.
- The next generation needs to develop their strengths. This can happen only if they are given some free rein to make mistakes.

Still, after years of being the head honcho, it can be difficult to let go. Here are some steps an owner can take to stand back and build up the next generation:

- **Allow the next generation to run with some ideas.** This must be done in an intelligent manner, of course. Start small, provide input, but let them run with it while making yourself available for help.

- **Encourage them.** As a regular course of business, major corporations like IBM conduct brainstorming sessions. Give employees advance notice that there will be such a session. Set the date, announce the rules, and commence.

The rules are: Don't allow criticism, encourage wild ideas, go for quantity, and combine and/or improve on others' ideas. The golden rule is that the owner must remain quiet. If you want to make it even better, have the next generation run the session. You can tee it up so that everyone knows you support it, but then leave the room.

Convey everything I have written here to the next generation, and declare this to be your goal. The next generation has been toiling under your tutelage for many years. At the beginning, it was pure command and control. Over time, some responsibilities were handed over, and the next generation may now be running certain parts of the company—heck, they may be running all of it. But they may be doing nothing more than cranking the crank the exact same way the first generation did for thirty years. The years of pounding into their brain "how it is done" has inherently suppressed parts of the brain that contemplate "how it *could* be done."

Ask the next generation to develop the strategic plan. In the field of family business and next generation prep work, there are multiple requirements that must be met to some degree for the next generation to be successful. The next to the last one is strategic development. What is the strategy over the next five, ten, twenty years? Placing this bombshell on the lap of the next generation can help to break them out of "follower" mode and move them into "leadership" mode.

Ask how they are going to significantly increase the revenue of the business. This is closely aligned to the strategic plan but has a sharper point on it. While the strategic plan meshes the company with the world around it, figuring out how to impact the revenue instills practicality in the process.

Implement ideas through pilots. Once you've opened Pandora's box, you may not be able to shut it again. No problem. If there is an idea out there, do a pilot—a small-scale version of the idea where you can validate whether the idea has real merit or not while minimizing risk and cost.

Innovation has been and always will be the game changer. It must be balanced with efficient operations. But the long-term success of your family business is predicated on creating an environment where the next generation has their antennas up and minds working on new ideas to improve and grow the business.

Logan Trading Company Just Keeps On Growing

Logan Trading Company is a highly successful garden center in the United States. It is also a third-generation family business that has seen its share of ups and downs but has managed to stay on course and thrive.

In 1965 Robert M. "Bob" Logan founded the company, primarily as a produce buyer. He quickly expanded his business to include selling garden products and brokering damaged railroad goods. Located in Raleigh, North Carolina, at the old Farmers Market off Capital Boulevard, his business grew, and he found that his success was centering on garden products.

Along the way, Bob and his wife, Helen, raised a large family: five girls and one boy named Robert M. Logan Jr. Like many family businesses, all the kids spent time working in the business. However, Robert remembers that his dad was always pressuring him to join the business full time. Robert thought he should be allowed to make up his own mind and pursue his own dream: joining the ministry. He enrolled in Southeastern Seminary.

While attending school he worked outside the business with his cousin doing landscaping. And during this time when he was not working for his father and was pursuing his own path, he had an epiphany: There are other ways to minister outside of being in the ministry, and he loved working with plants. In 1974, Robert decided to join his father full time.

In 1990, the state expanded the Farmers Market and moved it to another part of town. This did not sit well with Robert because it would take him too far from his current customer base. Scouring the area for a suitable location, he came across an abandoned railroad station near town.

The structure was in disrepair. Homeless people were living in it, and abandoned buildings surrounded it. There were weeds and overgrowth everywhere, it was near low-income housing, and noisy trains came through all the time. So not only would it take substantial money and effort to bring the site up to par, but also what customer in her right mind would want to shop here? His family and friends thought he was crazy—except for one.

Greg Poole and Bob had done some business in the past, and Robert had the opportunity to get to know Greg at an early age. By an amazing coincidence, or simply by providence, Greg approached Robert independently with an idea that he should relocate Logan's to the old railroad station and that he would help him do it.

So in 1991, with some hard work and a lot of advertising informing customers of the new location, Logan's opened its new store. Maybe two wrongs don't make a right, but just maybe two crazy people with vision make a genius.

The Family Problem

One of the top reasons family businesses fail is having too many shareholders. It is worse if many do not work in the business but have the majority ownership. Robert found himself in that situation when his father died in 1984. In essence, Bob had not been in full control of the business. In 2009, with family members getting older and Robert winning praise as the leader of the business, all the shares were consolidated underneath him.

He decided to close on Sundays, because it is a day of rest. Robert also decided to revive the old diner at the new location, and there has been a line for lunch ever since.

> **Dirty Little Secret:** One of the top reasons family businesses fail is having too many shareholders.

Robert and Julie have run Logan's over the years, and their two kids, Josh and Leslie, have grown up working in the business. However, based on Robert's philosophy of life, there is no pressure for his children to be a part of the business. He would rather they pursue their own dreams.

Josh wants to help underprivileged children in Brazil, and Leslie has a passion for music. Some years ago Josh was the general manager for Logan's, with Leslie working for him. Now Leslie is acting as general manager with Josh underneath her. It is looking like the Logan family tradition will continue into the next generation: Leslie and Josh will still be able to pursue their dreams, while providing a gardening oasis for their customers at the same time.

Keeping Sibling Relationships Positive and Productive

Perhaps you were not the only sibling to be given ownership of the company. I have a client with three second-generation family members in the business: one is the president and the others are vice presidents. How do they manage to get along, cooperate, and ensure the business is functioning at peak performance? It's tricky. Here are some strategies to keep your sibling relationships strong and your business moving forward.

Put the past behind you. Unfortunately, some adult siblings harbor resentment for events that happened when they were children, and they carry this baggage with them when dealing with their siblings. They pull these past incidents out as weapons whenever discussions get heated. It's similar to unhealthy marriages, where one partner pulls out the other's past misdeeds and wields them as weapons during an argument. These past misdeeds need to be addressed, forgiven, and put in the past for good. If you want to get along better with your brothers and sisters, you must do what is necessary to get past your childhood differences.

Open communication is the key. The next area of potential conflict comes when there is confusion over responsibilities. When siblings are acting like owners, they tend to jump in where needed. However, if everyone is jumping into today's problem, nothing else will get done. At the same time, if two people are separately working the same issue, there is redundancy of effort, wasted time, and ultimately frustration because only one solution to the problem can be used and the other loses out.

I believe the number-one factor in developing a good healthy sibling relationship in the workplace is communication. Organize regular meetings and allow siblings to put whatever they want on the agenda, including personal issues. Always leave time for discussion at the end for anyone to raise issues. Be sure to take turns leading the meetings. When conflict arises, practice active listening: Let the other people speak, then tell them what you believe was communicated, and ask if you understand correctly. It's important to understand that people cannot move on to the next logical point in a discussion if they're not convinced the other person has perfectly understood the previous point they were trying to make. And remember, understanding someone does not mean you agree, just that you understand.

Assure fair compensation. Another area that causes rifts in family business—you guessed it—money. How much is everyone getting paid? This is an issue particularly when it comes to siblings who are running the company, because there is no arbiter. Individual self-esteem and psychological makeup of the siblings are greatly affected by the unquestionable love and support received from their parents. Even though they may be completely different people, they're equal in the eyes of their mom and dad. But in the workplace, things don't work this way. The successful performance of the company is most important, and to a great extent, that performance comes from the people working there. The employees with better results will shoulder more responsibility and should have the appropriate title and compensation to go along with it.

The benefits, however, should be the same, including for family members who are not necessarily in the company. Think of a family's second home, for example. Dennis Jaffe, one of the great family business authors, believes the vacation home is a good indicator of family health. Who gets how many weeks? Is someone using it more than another? Does one want to sell? Does another always leave it a mess without fixing anything? It's easy to see how conflict could result, so it's important that the rules are the same for everyone. When it comes to the business, the big issue is vacation days.

Recognize long-term goals. As a final coping tip for working with your siblings, it is critical to have an understanding of each person's life goals and ambitions. Where do you want to be in five, ten, and fifteen years? Life changes a lot as you go through it. People get married and have kids, kids grow up, hobbies and passions come along, and good and bad life-altering events occur along the way.

As we go through life, our perspectives on what we want and need change. Check in with your siblings to see where they are on their path. Share your hopes and dreams for life with them. In doing so, you'll ensure you are all working together in a way that will allow each of you to get what you want and need out of the business and the family.

Four Must-Reads for Next-Generation Leaders

Hey next-generation leaders, you're about to get an educational crash course for success. This turbo boost requires you to read four books that will prepare you to be successful as a family business leader and in life.

Emotional Intelligence by Daniel Goleman

This first must-read covers the importance of emotional intelligence, a concept first coined by Daniel Goleman, who has since gone on to be declared a top-ten influential business thinker by the *Wall Street Journal*. In his book, Goleman describes how those who are most successful in business and life have a high degree of emotional intelligence—namely, self-awareness, emotional control, empathy, and the ability to influence others. Our societal structures dictate that to be successful we must make good grades in high school to get into a good college in order to get a good job. While this is still true, we have come to realize it's simply not enough; we must demonstrate emotional intelligence as well.

The 7 Habits of Highly Effective People by Stephen R. Covey

This highly acclaimed title from Stephen Covey covers the more traditional and fundamental skills and know-how required in business. You must read the book to really learn all seven, but the overall concept is to structure your behavior so that you will be successful. Habit number 1, *be proactive*, makes the most impact, I believe. Think about this. Most of us in the workplace are passive. We can do it tomorrow or simply react when a problem or opportunity arises. Along the same lines as being proactive is to "do it now." If you have decided a course of action, ask yourself, "Why can't I implement this decision right now, today, this very moment?" Many times, you will find there is no reason why you can't start today. No, it won't be perfect, but speed conquers perfection. Don't confuse being proactive with being busy. This is a major mental fallacy; simply being busy or doing physically taxing work is not being proactive.

Habit number 5 is *first understand, and then be understood*. Convince the speaker that you understand, and then you can convey your point. If done like this, others will hear your point instead of focusing on trying to get you to understand theirs. Family businesses are breeding grounds for conflict. Manage it with effective communication. Habit number 7 is *sharpen the saw*—never stop learning, growing, and accepting change.

Kids, Wealth, and Consequences
by Richard A. Morris and Jayne A. Pearl

Family businesses are businesses that families own. Thus, Mom and Dad set the direction and direct employees on their course of action. They are in control and have the power to hire and fire people. The livelihood of the employees is in their control. Moreover, as owners, Mom and Dad reap the benefits of the profits. This environment can have a psychological effect on the next generation in that they

(continued)

may come to believe they're superior to those around them due to the family's power and wealth. Or they may think simply that they're the children of the people in charge. In actual fact, the parents' position of power has come about through extremely long, hard, and smart work. This book guides you, as the next generation, through financial, intellectual, and spiritual/emotional choices to assist your development into a well-balanced adult.

How many family businesses get into trouble because someone in the family thought they deserved what they hadn't earned? There is a family business in which a father handed his business down to his two sons, naming one president. Unfortunately, the president was driving the business into the ground while ignoring the input from his father and brother. When this son decided to default on a company buyout payment, the dad had no choice but to seize the company back.

Steve Jobs by Walter Isaacson

Rounding out this portfolio of must-reads for next-generation business leaders is the biography about Steve Jobs, the late cofounder of Apple. This book is a massive case study of the earlier three books, and far beyond them. Let me be clear here: It is not a book on how it's done, but rather it shows the good and the bad. The author says Jobs told him to write whatever he wanted, and Jobs put no constraints on it. This is probably the first time Jobs ever did that, and you can immediately see that it's true. Jobs's behavior through much of his life, as chronicled in the book, was nothing less than abhorrent—not to deny that he was a creative genius who brought the world many wonderful things.

It is a full exposé on leadership styles, interaction, and effectiveness. It is unparalleled on motivation, innovation, and creativity. It covers multiple aspects found in the books *Emotional Intelligence* and *The 7 Habits of Highly Effective People*. I would contend that the Jobs biography will soon become required reading at some of the top business schools around the world.

You'll notice that these reading suggestions aren't hardcore family business books. One deals with family and wealth, but the others have no direct family content. That's because the major elements of success for you, as the next-generation family business leader, are more fundamental: Have feelings, be structured, earn your way, and have passion, even if you have to break the rules sometimes.

Don't Ignore the Need for Self-Improvement in a Family Business

The dynamics of family businesses are complex and have broad reverberations. If you have managed to work your way through this minefield and have succeeded in passing the torch to the next generation, you can consider yourself a gold medal winner in the family business competition. However, the race does not end there.

When I worked for IBM, there was an understanding that all employees should make a concerted effort to improve themselves. There were courses available inside and outside the company, an extensive library, and compensation to purchase business books. Self-improvement was so expected that "personal development" was part of everyone's annual performance review.

Yes, I understand that a multibillion-dollar company can afford to allocate such resources to employee improvement. But this is missing the point: Personal development is important. And for family businesses, it is easily forgotten, ignored, or put aside.

Family businesses tend to be insular. Most are privately held and thus are not held to the same reporting standards as a publicly traded company. More relevant is that most of the critical data and information is reserved for the inner circle—the owners, founders, and/or family. This attitude of not letting information out of the inner circle creates a similar myopia about letting outside information in. Indeed, this insularity, particularly if the company has been successful in the past, can create a belief and mindset that the business philosophy of the inner circle is superior to anything else out there, and external information and counsel are shunned.

[N]ot letting information out of the inner circle creates a similar myopia about letting outside information in.

Some of this is justifiable, if you truly are the market leader. However, there is a difference between ignoring outside education, advice, and information, and bringing it in, evaluating it, and determining which parts may be useful and which are not.

We met with members of a family business a few years back to discuss how we might provide help. After a couple of hours it became clear that both the family and the business were highly functioning and succession was proceeding smoothly with everyone on board. We determined that they did not need any help and applauded them for having a discipline to always be on the lookout for ways to improve.

Look at Jack Welch, ex-CEO of GE and considered a great leader of one of the great businesses. Nevertheless, while at the helm of GE, he retained a personal business consultant to keep him on his toes. If one of the greatest leaders of an iconic company needs help, don't you?

So you are the new leader of the family business, but the transition has occurred rather early. As such, there may be some experiences and perspectives you need to gain in order to fully equip yourself to be a successful leader in the future. For example, here are some questions to ask: Are you truly willing to accept constructive criticism? Are you willing to admit when you are wrong or have made a mistake? Have you dealt with conflict? Have you been in a situation requiring perseverance? Are you a good listener?

These are experiences and attitudes common to good business leadership. If you are already at this point and consider yourself a fairly well-seasoned leader, do you take seriously the concept of continual personal development? Do you read self-help business and industry books? Take coursework specific to your industry? Belong to leadership groups like Vistage or YPO? Do you spend some time with a business coach? Have a network of mentors? Attend Toastmasters to improve your public speaking? Participate in business groups like the Chamber or Rotary?

If you are a new family business leader, you may believe

that you have sufficient experience and education, and the success of the business proves it. Or you may think that you are too small, too busy, or don't have the resources to spend time improving yourself. You would be wrong on both counts.

On Managing Millennials

When I present at conferences, people always ask for my advice on how to deal with millennials. The sentiment seems to be that millennials drive everyone a little crazy. So, I wanted to address this for you. At a high level, while we do need to find a way to hold millennials more accountable, I believe family business owners can also begin to improve things by first seeking to better understand the millennials in their companies, learning how to take advantage of the smarts and tech savvy of next generation.

Every generation has issues with the next and vice versa. Baby boomers (those born between 1946 and 1964), for example, approach things differently and operate out of a distinctive context. They come from a world of sacrifice, loyalty, hard work, and dependability, much of it formed from their proximity to World War II and perhaps even stories they heard about the Great Depression. My own mother kept cash under her mattress in case the world fell apart again.

Millennials, on the other hand, though they have likely heard similar stories from their grandparents, have not been directly affected by these world events in the same way that baby boomers were. There's a natural disconnect. While baby boomers are generally always ready for the bottom to fall out of things or to expect consequences to be dire, millennials seem to respond to potentially serious business situations by saying thinks like "Don't worry," "It will be okay," or "It doesn't matter." It could be that, on some level, they're ignorant of the consequences of the situation. It could be that they're demonstrating a lack of respect. But I think there may be more to it than that.

Not only is this generation of millennials different from the ones that preceded it, but I would contend that things in our culture and world have changed so quickly and deeply that they are barely recognizable. In the New York Times best-selling book, Factfulness: Ten Reasons We're Wrong about the World—and Why Things Are Better Than You Think, authors Hans Rosling, Anna Rosling Rönnlund, and Ola Rosling, discuss instincts that distort people's perspectives about the world. Interestingly, their book shows how we tend to incorrectly answer simple questions about global trends, and the authors say that we do this so systematically that even a monkey answering the same questions at random could outperform thousands of well-educated respondents from around the globe. Did you know, for example:

- The number of children dying before the age of 5 has dropped from about 40% in 1900 to 4% worldwide?
- World hunger has dropped from 28% in 1970 to 11% in 2015?
- Plane crash deaths dropped from 2,100 per 10 billion miles in the 1930s to 1 between the years 2010 to 2016?
- The number of movies per year has increased from about 1,000 in 1960 to over 11,000 today?
- New music has increased from thousands in the 1960s to over 6 million today?

- The number of science articles per year has increased from thousands in 1950 to over two million today?
- The number of people with mobile phones has increased from less than .001 percent in 1980 to over 65% in more recent years?
- The number of people using the Internet has increased from 0% in 1980 to almost 50% today?
- Playable guitars per million people has increased from only 200 in 1962 to over 11,000 today?

The world has changed more in the last fifty years than at any other time in history. If you are a baby boomer, what is going on in the world could possibly be passing you by. Is your brain, mentality, and view of the world so grounded in an old world paradigm that you could potentially be unaware of how things have changed?

Have you ever heard the saying about Latin American soccer players? This is the idea that since they are born with a soccer ball at their feet, it's no wonder they are so good. Borrowing this concept, if you were to try kicking a soccer ball for the first time at age 25, it can be assumed you might not be at the same level as someone who has been playing all their life. Consider that baby boomers or those of other similar generations might *think* they're up to speed but really are functioning from a whole different perspective and set of experiences.

Generally speaking, millennials were born with computers, the Internet, and mobile phones at their fingertips. And though your kid may be good at Snapchatting on his iPhone that still may not translate into great business behavior. But with the world beneath our feet changing so rapidly, it's no wonder we may struggle to understand millennials. How can we figure this out so that we bring out the best in one another, appreciating what each of us brings to the table? Let's take a quick look into the brain of a millennial.

The Millennial Brain

What millennials value most is the attractiveness of the work itself, mobility (both geographical and between assignments), the opportunity to meet people and network, and a relaxed atmosphere. They love being able to customize their compensation packages with things like additional days off, flexible hours, telecommuting, or discounts. Additionally:

1. **Millennials believe in work/life balance.** Unlike the family business, the next generation views life and work as two separate entities—and life comes before work. Millennials don't view it as work/life balance but rather life/work balance.

2. **Millennials view being inclusive as vital.** They value teamwork and their teammates. They give preference to relationships at any level and expect ready access to those in positions of influence.

3. **Millennials are goal-oriented but in a way that differs from boomers and Gen Xers.** They can be impatient and thrive on quick results. Millennials were brought up in a fast-paced, hectic environment.

4. **Millennials want feedback in real time.** For next generation millennials, feedback is informal and expected throughout the day. For family business boomer managers, this can feel draining.

5. **Millennials want to fit the culture and for the culture**

to fit them. This is imperative for them. Culture trumps money when it comes to motivating millennials.

How to Better Manage Millennials

Millennials often get a bad rap. They are lumped together with other millennials and judged as a group. And like any group, they are not all alike. However, trends do emerge.

To better manage millennials, creating a strong company culture is key. For them, culture and core values should be in line with their own ideals and lifestyle. Here are six ways to properly integrate millennials into the culture of your organization:

1. **Create a collaborative working environment.** There is a stereotype that millennials are demanding. In truth, millennials have an urge to contribute. Encourage collaboration in your company by holding weekly team meetings or brainstorming sessions. Listen to what millennials have to say.

2. **Encourage the use of tech and social media.** Take advantage of the tech savvy of millennials. They function in networked environments where simultaneous communications are more efficient than long meetings. Never try to deny them the use of technology because this can be a flash point with millennials.

3. **Create a future that gets them excited.** Lay out the future vision and talk about their career path. Perhaps get the millennials involved in family governance. If you share with them the reason that something must be done, they may surprise you with ideas about how to achieve it.

4. **Make work fun.** Fun matters. Millennials are extremely enthusiastic and optimistic, and they crave a work environment that fosters their outgoing attitude. They are more willing to do hard work when it's in a fun environment.

5. **Let them know how they are doing before they ask you.** This is a feedback generation. Millennials thrive on feedback and expect routine encouragement. The absence of feedback could be interpreted to mean that you do not value them.

6. **Do not micromanage their methods.** Give them space to learn, discover, and experiment. Millennials like a challenge and the chance to create innovative solutions. Let them learn through immersion, engagement, trial and error, and entrepreneurial activities.

Where You Don't Bend for Millennials

It's important to acknowledge that the world is changing and to try to accommodate the millennial mindset. However, there are areas in business that just can't be compromised. At a minimum, certain basic and sound business practices have been true since the beginning of time and they continue to apply today:

- Follow through with a commitment.
- Take responsibility for your actions and mistakes.
- All actions in the business must be made with an eye towards "How does this make the company profitable?"
- Good business decisions, even when gut decisions

need to be made, should still always be based on some form of data, history, or research.

- Good personal relationships and communication with employees, customers, and suppliers is paramount.
- Have a reputation of trustworthiness, integrity, dependability, and respect for others.
- Always be a student of your field, and consistently strive for excellence.

Advice to Millennials: How to Handle Baby Boomers

If you've read the preceding paragraphs, you really already have your answer. And if you truly want to one day take over the family business, you are going to need to demonstrate that you are competent with the current business and system, even though it may be old, archaic, and dysfunctional to you. Stand in your parent's shoes. Try to see where they are coming from. Once they know that you get their point of view, and the best way to do this is through active listening, and you have demonstrated a level of competence, they will better be able to take seriously the changes you would like to make.

The family business is not the place to come to show how cool you are with technology or how many ideas you can generate in order to make the business better. There are a lot of moving parts in a business, a lot is at stake, and there is a lot of history. While it can be profoundly difficult to get parents or those of other generations to evolve as quickly as they should (they may stay longer than needed), you need to bring them along as best you can.

The Good News About Millennials

While there are many behaviors and attitudes about millennials that frustrate baby boomers, there is a glimmer of good news. Many of you have perhaps heard of something called the marshmallow test. This was an experiment that consisted of a series of studies on delayed gratification in the late 1960s and early 1970s, led by psychologist Walter Mischel, who was then a professor at Stanford University.

In these studies, a child was offered a choice between one small reward that would be provided immediately or instead two small rewards if they would be wiling to wait for a short period, during which the tester left the room and then returned. The reward was sometimes a marshmallow (or a cookie or pretzel.) In follow-up studies, researchers found that the children who were able to wait longer for the preferred rewards tended to have better life outcomes, as later indicated by their SAT scores, levels of educational attainment, body mass index (BMI), and other life measures.

Here is the good news for you: These tests were rerun in the 1990s and 2000s, and the results showed that, for some reason, more kids are opting to wait and are waiting longer.

"What's striking is that nearly 60 percent of preschoolers tested in the 2000s waited out the entire 10-minute delay period, versus almost 40 percent in the 1980s and about 30 percent in the 1960s," says Duke psychologist Avshalom Caspi.[2]

So, if millennials are grasping the importance of delayed gratification better than kids born in the 1960s, and delayed

---

2 Bower, Bruce. "Kids today are waiting longer than ever in the classic marshmallow test." Science News 194, no. 3 (August 4, 2018): 14.

gratification is correlated with having better life outcomes, then maybe, just maybe, millennials will turn out alright in the end.

Conclusion

There can be no greater joy than successfully owning and running a business where you get to work with the people you love the most. At the same time it can be lucrative and provide a fulfilling life. Unfortunately there are many obstacles that impede so many family businesses from achieving this.

Most often, it is the inherent blending of business with family. Business is a bottom-line, profit-driven, no-holds-barred competition to perform and evolve better than your competitors in providing products and services to the marketplace at a value point that customers are willing to pay for, and to generate sufficient profit at the end of the day. Families are the exact opposite—they are a broader extension of who we are as individuals. It is our clan, it is our core group, it is where we always belong, it is our refuge, and it is our home. And it cannot be changed.

Family businesses go awry when they are unsuccessful in maintaining adequate balance between the demands of the business and the needs of the family. Family businesses are like a bicycle—if one wheel is not operating fully, then the entire enterprise does not properly function. We must pay sufficient homage to both sides of the equation, each of which has polar opposite requirements. Moreover, while there is certainly an art to being successful in business, dealing with relationships is a fuzzier and more amorphous issue to tackle. This is probably why so many family businesses are now reaching out for help.

> **Dirty Little Secret:** Family businesses go awry when they are unsuccessful in maintaining adequate balance between the demands of the business and the needs of the family.

The purpose of this book is to enable those family members connected to a family business to get a deeper look at the underlying mechanics of what makes a family business work and not work, which are not typically discussed at cocktail parties. As mentioned at the beginning of the book, every family is different, and thus the answers to successfully moving forward, while there are certainly some best practices, are unique to each family. The cookie-cutter approach is wholly ineffective. I am hopeful that some information contained in *Dirty Little Secrets of Family Business* resonated with you and your family business.

We have covered a lot of ground, and now I would like to leave you with two big-picture perspectives for when the water level seems to be rising too high to bear. These perspectives will help you clear your head and keep moving forward.

Your employees—especially ones who have been around for a while, the senior ones, and the really good ones—know what many of the issues are. However, they are not going to tell you. They know that speaking the truth could put their jobs in jeopardy, now or somewhere down the road. At the same time, family members—especially longtime owners—are mostly unable to hear about the issues from an employee. It is an "emperor has no clothes" situation.

When you find yourself wound up in knots trying to figure out how to solve a complex and seemingly intractable family business situation, try to step back and, for a moment, imagine that none of these people are related to each other. Now how would you solve the problem? This perspective can provide enormous clarity. This is not necessarily the answer, but it can assist greatly in constructing a solution that ultimately works for you, the business, and the family.

Appendix 1: Online Family Business Assessment

I hope you have enjoyed reading *Dirty Little Secrets of Family Business* but more importantly, have learned some things that will help you improve yourself and your family business. Our goal at Family Business USA is to educate, train, and advise family business members to preserve the wealth they have built up in their business and to maintain family harmony.

Further to this, we have created an Online Family Business Assessment. Go to **FamilyBusinessUSA.com/FBA**, answer the test questions posed, and our team will perform an analysis of the data and provide you with an assessment of your family business situation, at no cost.

About the Author

Henry Hutcheson, Certified Management Consultant®, Certified Family Business Advisor is the founder and president of Family Business USA and specializes in helping family businesses and privately held businesses ensure profitability, prepare for transition, secure wealth, and strengthen family relationships.

With twenty-five years of business management and family business consulting experience, he has successfully helped families across the United States and internationally, and in a broad range of industries. While his focus is on succession, his work entails managing conflict and enhancing communication, planning and preparing the family and business for a smooth transition to the next generation, grooming the next generation as high-performance leaders, and working with the exiting generation to define their role going forward.

Henry grew up working for his family's business, Olan Mills Portrait Studios; had an international management career with IBM, UPS, and Sumitomo Electric; and now works with family businesses across the globe.

He studied psychology in Switzerland, has a BA from the University of Texas at Austin, and earned an MBA from Columbia Business School. He is a Certified Family Business Advisor (CFBA), a Certified Management Consultant (CMC), serves on the board of the Carolinas chapter of the Institute of Management Consultants, and is a past regional board member of the Society of Financial Services Professionals. He is also a member of the Family Firm Institute.

Henry is a frequent speaker at professional, university, and corporate-sponsored events; was a family business columnist for the *News & Observer* and the *Charlotte Observer* newspapers; and is the current family business columnist for the national magazine *Nursery Retailer* and the Columbia newspaper *The State*. He has written for *Family Business Magazine* and has been quoted in the *Wall Street Journal* and *Crain's*, as well as in various business and trade magazines across the country. He has also been quoted in two family business–related books: *Kids, Wealth, and Consequences* and *Sink or Swim: How Lessons from the Titanic Can Save Your Family Business*.

Made in United States
North Haven, CT
14 February 2023

32541933R00150